The New York Times

PUBLIC PROFILES

LeBron James

THE NEW YORK TIMES EDITORIAL STAFF

Published in 2020 by New York Times Educational Publishing in association with The Rosen Publishing Group, Inc. 29 East 21st Street, New York, NY 10010

First Edition

The New York Times
Alex Ward: Editorial Director, Book Development
Phyllis Collazo: Photo Rights/Permissions Editor
Heidi Giovine: Administrative Manager

Rosen Publishing
Megan Kellerman: Managing Editor
Danielle Weiner: Editor
Greg Tucker: Creative Director
Brian Garvey: Art Director

Cataloging-in-Publication Data
Names: New York Times Company.
Title: LeBron James / edited by the New York Times editorial staff.
Description: New York : New York Times Educational Publishing, 2020. | Series: Public profiles | Includes glossary and index.
Identifiers: ISBN 9781642822489 (library bound) | ISBN 9781642822472 (pbk.) | ISBN 9781642822496 (ebook)
Subjects: LCSH: James, LeBron—Juvenile literature. | Basketball players—United States—Biography—Juvenile literature. | African American basketball players—Biography—Juvenile literature.
Classification: LCC GV884.J36 L437 2020 | DDC 796.323092 B—dc23

Manufactured in the United States of America

On the cover: A fan in a combination of LeBron James jerseys from the Cavaliers and Lakers at Quicken Loans Arena in Cleveland, Nov. 21, 2018; Ash Adams for The New York Times.

Contents

Moves, Basketball and Otherwise

CHAPTER 3

Criticism and Challenges

CHAPTER 4

On the Political Court

CHAPTER 5

Personality and Pursuits

Introduction

LEBRON JAMES WAS famous before he graduated high school. He led his team at St. Vincent-St. Mary High School to three Ohio state championships. His games drew crowds, and both Nike and Adidas were already courting him for sponsorships prior to his senior year. Early in his life, James knew he wanted to be in the N.B.A. When the time came, he handled the media attention with the maturity and responsibility of one realizing a long-sought goal. On only a handful of occasions has James misstepped. Well into his career, he is one of the most highly ranked, valued and admired basketball players of all time.

LeBron James's professional lifestyle seemed inevitable. Before his senior year of high school, he appeared on the cover of Sports Illustrated. The magazine dubbed him "The Chosen One," a name reserved for the player that would lead a new generation of All-Stars and bring back national interest to the N.B.A. The nickname stuck, and James would live up to it. The attention surrounding James was so widespread, and his success was so certain, that both Adidas and Nike offered him endorsement deals after he graduated high school. James signed a $90 million, seven-year deal with Nike, the largest single-player deal in the company's history.

In 2003, LeBron James was drafted to the N.B.A. by the Cleveland Cavaliers, a then-struggling franchise that had the first pick of the draft. That season, James won the Rookie of the Year award, the first team member from the Cleveland Cavaliers and the youngest in N.B.A. history to do so. While James did not win any titles with the Cavaliers, he helped them improve their standing in the Eastern Conference, and continued to garner recognition for his own abilities.

LeBron James after an interview at the U.C.L.A. Health Training Center during Media Day for the Los Angeles Lakers, Sept. 24, 2018.

James was eligible to become a free agent in 2010, after seven years and two contracts with the Cleveland Cavaliers. He announced he would be taking his talents to the Miami Heat, in a move that upset many Clevelanders. Fans expressed disappointment and anger, but the most scathing reaction was perhaps an open letter written by the Cavaliers majority owner, Dan Gilbert, denouncing James's decision. Yet James's career soared with the Miami Heat. He won two Championship titles and, at 28 years old, became the youngest player in N.B.A. history to score 20,000 points, surpassing Kobe Bryant, who previously held the record at 29 years old.

After five seasons with the Miami Heat, LeBron James chose to become a free agent once again. This time, he returned to Cleveland, earning forgiveness from his previously angered fans. James cited his desire to bring a championship title to Cleveland, as well as to invest in his hometown of Akron, Ohio, as reasons for his return in an emotional but understated press conference. LeBron's presence in Cleveland bolstered the economy and overall morale. James made the choice out of a deepening connection to his roots and a desire to have a positive impact on the area in which he grew up. In 2016, during his second season back with the Cavaliers, James succeeded in winning the championship title.

In 2018, James became a free agent yet again. This time, he joined the Los Angeles Lakers. The move garnered mixed reactions. On the one hand, James's exiting Cleveland did not spark the anger it had in 2010. Critics instead focused on whether or not James was title-hungry, but James addressed this in press interviews and allayed their judgment. He expressed a desire to grow with the Lakers as a team rather than as a title-seeker.

James has largely avoided controversy throughout his career. But since the 2016 presidential election, James has participated in online banter aimed at President Donald J. Trump. Prior to the election, James endorsed Secretary Hillary Clinton for office, stating that she was the candidate who could understand the struggle of children growing up as he did, in communities with little resources and support. Since President Trump entered office, James has taken offense at several of the president's comments, deeming them racist. He and the president interacted via Twitter, and the negative feelings appeared to be mutual.

James himself is taking action to provide support for children growing up in his hometown. In 2018, James opened an elementary school in his hometown of Akron and continued to be invested in the activities of the LeBron James Family foundation. The I Promise School is a revolutionary public elementary and secondary school, catering to students with test scores below grade level. The school offers wraparound services to students and their families, such as food pantries and eyeglasses, to ensure that students are able to succeed in the classroom. LeBron James's charitable activities have come to define his character in the public eye.

CHAPTER 1

The Chosen One

LeBron James's career rests on the foundation of his childhood and adolescence in Akron, Ohio. He attended St. Vincent-St. Mary High School, where he quickly became a basketball star, leading his team to two Division III State Championship titles. His high school nickname, King James, would follow him throughout his career. After landing on the cover of Sports Illustrated prior to his senior year, James also became known as The Chosen One, the player who would usher in a new All-Star era. Despite controversy over a potential OHSAA violation, James handled the media attention with grace and maturity.

It's Decisions, Decisions for LeBron James

BY BRANDON LILLY | JULY 12, 2002

FINALLY, ON THE FOURTH day of the Adidas ABCD camp at Fairleigh Dickinson University, the one-man circus that is LeBron James came to town.

James, who is entering his senior year of high school in Akron, Ohio, is considered to be the top schoolboy basketball player in the country. He strolled into his news conference this morning wearing a T-shirt that said "King James" on the front with his No. 23, just in case the reporters gathered here forgot whom they were talking to.

But his appearance was not really about basketball, since he was not playing because of a broken wrist he sustained in June during a charity game in Chicago. Instead, this was a business trip. Having spent the first part of the week at the Nike camp in Indianapolis, James came to the Adidas camp today in part not to show favoritism to either side in the growing battle by the two sneaker giants to obtain his promotional services if he declares for the N.B.A. draft next spring.

"Of course, this is a business thing," James said. "I don't have any favorites right now. When they're ready to make a decision they can come at me with deals and then my family and I will sit down to make a decision. I haven't signed a contract with anybody yet. I wear whatever I want."

For Dru Joyce, James's coach at St. Vincent-St. Mary High School in Akron, seeing James attract this kind of attention has become commonplace.

Two of James's high school teammates, Romeo Travis and Joyce's son, who is also named Dru, were invited to the camp in large part because of James's celebrity status. Joyce himself was invited as a coach.

"It's a little bit overwhelming at times, and I wish there was a book I could have read as far as dealing with this type of media crush before I took the job," said Joyce, who is in his second year as head coach at James's high school. "For right now, I am just enjoying the ride, and next year when he leaves I can sink back into some sort of anonymity."

James does not expect to be able to play for at least another three weeks, but he hopes to be able to participate in the Michael Jordan camp in Santa Barbara, Calif., early next month. But it won't be the only time James visits the West Coast this year.

St. Vincent-St. Mary will meet the California high school powerhouse Mater Dei at U.C.L.A.'s Pauley Pavilion in December, part of an extensive tour for St. Vincent-St. Mary. James's team will also play in Philadelphia; Trenton; Chapel Hill, N.C.; Cleveland; and Columbus, Ohio, all in the span of six weeks.

But for event promoters, an appearance by James does not come cheap.

Bobby Jacobs, who coordinates the Slam Dunk to the Beach Tournament in Delaware and featured James and St. Vincent-St. Mary last year, said the asking price for the Irish has tripled this spring, jumping from $5,000 to almost $15,000.

But despite all the hype, James seems remarkably unaffected. With his mother, Gloria James, by his side, he said all the right things at his news conference, careful not to divulge much, but doing so in a very professional manner. He said college is still an option for him, and again listed North Carolina, Duke, Louisville, Florida and Ohio State as his favorites. Only once did he perhaps let his intentions slip.

"When I was in the fifth grade, I wrote down my career goals, and one of them was to be in the N.B.A.," he said. "My teachers would tell me I was crazy but I never changed it. I look forward to being there next year.

"Or the year after that," he added.

Hoops in Hollywood, for Young Dreamers

BY MIKE WISE | JAN. 5, 2003

BEFORE THE BIG GAME at Pauley Pavilion last night, there was the big luncheon in Beverly Hills on Friday, replete with prime rib, Yorkshire pudding and pretournament gossip.

Darryl Strawberry Jr., the son of the former star major league outfielder, would have the part-time job of guarding LeBron James, the guy expected to go No. 1 in June's N.B.A. draft. After the usual welcomes and pleasantries from organizers, all the cameramen and the reporters followed the players and the coaches into an adjacent room, hanging on their every utterance.

"You're not going to stop LeBron James, nobody can," said Strawberry, known as D. J. "I just hope to get help and maybe contain him a little."

Did we mention D. J. is 17?

For better or for worse, high school hoops went Hollywood last night. James's team, St. Vincent-St. Mary of Akron, Ohio, beat Southern California's perennial powerhouse, Mater Dei, 64-58, in something called the Dream Classic. ESPN2 televised it.

In front of a sellout crowd, James was special at times, swatting a 6-foot-9 player's shot against the glass, converting two alley-oop layups and distributing several dazzling assists. He also missed a lot of long jumpers, picked up three offensive fouls and was never able to dunk. He had 21 points, 9 rebounds, 7 assists and 3 blocked shots, making 8 of 24 shots and 7 turnovers.

Not bad for America's most prominent blue-chip star, but the standards are already ridiculously high.

"A lot of people are criticizing high school kids being on TV, but as for me, I feel we should be on TV," said Sebastian Telfair, whose Lincoln High Railsplitters made the trip from Brooklyn and played in the late, nontelevised game. "Everybody wants to be on TV."

What high school player wouldn't? After all the debate, you wonder: is it the LeBron phenomenon or our insatiable need to rush teenagers along?

The crowd tonight featured Mitch Kupchak, the Los Angeles Lakers' general manager, and his Sacramento Kings counterpart, Geoff Petrie. Kupchak went to a high school tournament in Las Vegas several years ago, feeling guilty that part of his job had become scouting 14- and 15-year-olds. But now, he concedes, it's part of the landscape.

When Gary McKnight, the longtime Mater Dei coach, said, "I think people love the fanfare and the innocence of high school basketball, where they play for lettermen's jackets and cheerleaders," he probably missed the representatives from Adidas and Nike, who are waging about a $20 million competition for James's endorsement. They sat under one basket last night, separated by Mater Dei cheerleaders, hoping beyond hope that James would sign with their sneaker company.

High school legends today also play for the people who outfit their schools, and for online rating services like HoopScoop, whose editor, Clark Francis, saw Telfair play in fourth grade. "I've got seven sixth-graders ranked right now," Francis said. "These kids love this stuff."

Innocence? Dime magazine featured Telfair with several women in a recent issue. Telfair thought the photo shoot was a good idea at the time, but now realizes he probably should not have agreed to pose. As cutting-edge glossy publications go, Dime and its soft-core porn make Slam magazine look like a Chip Hilton novel.

"What some people see as fun, others see as bad judgment," Telfair said. "I should have seen that." That's the problem. These youngsters have to think for themselves because we're too caught up in their talent to think for them anymore.

Make no mistake, beneath the diamond-encrusted crucifix and earrings James wore on Friday — "They only cost 25 cents in a gumball machine," he said with a straight face — the gold ropes, the Cadillac Escalades with the woofers booming, they are still youngsters who hunt for the occasional authority figure amid the mass of autograph seekers.

Once, long ago, elite high school teams would be invited to a holiday tournament, and they would make do with a little meal money and attend the tournament banquet at the host school's cafeteria. If the tournament was in Los Angeles, they would try to take in Disneyland.

Now, Dinos Trigonis, the event's promoter, hopes to gross more than $100,000 — most of which he says will go to charity. Every rabid hoop fan knows which player can go to his left, who can meet the grade and whose parents are too meddlesome.

As for the life-altering field trip as a youngster, that's their fathers' world. These players have been on the circuit for years. Several of the Mater Dei players beat James and some of his teammates at an A.A.U. national championship tournament in Orlando, Fla. — as eighth graders. The Mater Dei players were actually asked by a reporter if playing against James at 14 gave them confidence coming into the game, as if he somehow skipped adolescence.

But they are growing so fast and getting so good so young; that is where we are now, out of sorts and out of perspective.

"I blame A.A.U. for a lot of this," James said. "We've been to Tennessee, Florida, Utah. We've been everywhere. When we go to Italy, it might be different."

At the postgame news conference, James's coach, Dru Joyce, bristled when a reporter asked whether his players had missed any school.

When the reporter said he was sorry for having the gumption to broach the subject of schoolwork to a high school student, James said: "I've got a 3.3 right now. I'm straight."

James, a few months shy of a pro contract, would never have played here in one of college basketball's most storied arenas if not for last night's game. But do not expect him to grow nostalgic about

John Wooden's great U.C.L.A. teams or walk around the campus awestruck.

"All business," he said.

Funny, no? It takes the kids to be honest about what went on in Westwood last night.

The LeBron James Show Is Coming to the End of Act I

BY BILL FINLEY | MARCH 27, 2003

LEBRON JAMES WAS BOOED.

James, the 18-year-old who is expected to be the No. 1 pick in the N.B.A. draft in June, was alone underneath his basket in the McDonald's all-American game with 9 minutes 5 seconds to play and dunked ever so gently, with no flair, menace or thunder. He merely scored, not acceptable to the 18,728 at Gund Arena who came not necessarily to watch a high school all-star game, but to see the LeBron James Show.

Such is life when you are bigger than the game.

It was all about James tonight, not the final score or the other 23 very talented players. James's East team defeated the West, 122-107, and he led all scorers with 27 points, falling 4 points short of Jonathan Bender's record.

No surprise, James was named the game's most valuable player. And except for the slam that was not much of a slam, most everything he did was worthy of the highlight reel.

"I'm not trying to do things for the crowd," the 6-foot-8 James said, his array of dunks and no-look passes notwithstanding. "I'm trying to play for my teammates and coaches. When I play my game, we usually come away with a win. I'd say I played pretty well tonight."

James is in limbo, not really a high school player, not yet an N.B.A. millionaire. This was his first game since leading St. Vincent-St. Mary of Akron, Ohio, to its third state title in four years. He will play in two more high school all-star games, the Roundball Classic in Chicago on Monday and the Jordan Capital Classic in Washington on April 17.

As he did here, James will no doubt attract huge crowds. Tonight's attendance set a record for the 26-year-old McDonald's game.

At media day on Tuesday, James did not show up initially, and reporters were told he was granting interviews only to three television programs and a syndicated radio show. Later, when James did appear before a full contingent of news media, event organizers said the reporters could ask only about basketball and specifically the McDonald's game; they said the request came from James's family.

Reporters were told that if their questions veered from the allowable subjects, they could lose their credentials.

There were no such restrictions after the game, but James shed little light on his future. Asked where he expected to be playing at this time next year, he said: "I really don't know. God will lead me in the best direction and I will follow his footsteps."

News accounts earlier this winter indicated that James was unhappy with the Cleveland Cavaliers after they fired Coach John Lucas. It was Lucas who included James in a voluntary workout for the Cavaliers in 2002. The N.B.A. later fined the team $150,000 for including an under-age player in an N.B.A. workout.

James seems to have mellowed on the subject of the Cavaliers, who have the worst record in the N.B.A. and stand an excellent chance of winning the lottery for the No. 1 pick — and, presumably, James.

"My lifetime goal has been to play in the N.B.A. someday," he said. "It would be great to stay at home, but only God knows where I'll wind up."

Unless he decides to go to college, which no one expects, he is no longer under any amateur restrictions. He can sign with an agent, accept free throwback jerseys and sign a sneaker contract. (Nike is expected to beat out Adidas for the right to peddle LeBron James shoes.) He must declare for the N.B.A. draft by May 12.

Tonight, some of James's flashier plays involved behind-the-back or no-look passes to teammates for dunks. On one play, he purposely bounced the ball off the backboard to Charlie Villanueva of Blair Academy in Blairstown, N.J., whose dunk brought the crowd to its feet. James finished with seven assists.

"Early, I wanted to get my teammates comfortable and into the flow," James said. "A lot of them had never played in front of a crowd like this and they were nervous. I tried to give them the ball and get them comfortable. When the West team started to make a comeback, my teammates said, 'We know that you have scoring ability, try to take over.' "

At times James scored at will, but everything was from inside eight feet. He shot 12 for 24 but was 0 for 5 on 3-pointers.

It mattered little. He was just supposed to be exceptional and more special than anyone else. In that regard, he did not disappoint.

James Era Begins Before 15,123

BY CHARLIE NOBLES | JULY 9, 2003

LEBRON JAMES, PLAYING his first game in a Cleveland Cavaliers' uniform, drew close to a capacity crowd at the Orlando Magic's home court tonight and turned in a 14-point effort marked by several scintillating plays.

Afterward, he said that maintaining stamina was his biggest immediate challenge.

"The courts are way longer than the high school courts I played on," said James, who had 7 rebounds and 6 assists to go with his double-digit scoring in 23 minutes as a group of young Cavaliers defeated the Orlando Magic's young players, 107-80.

Ten of James's points came in the first quarter as the Cavaliers built a 19-point halftime lead. But over all, his first game for the Cavaliers turned what is normally a nondescript summer league game into a showcase for basketball's most discussed player.

The Magic has always played its summer league games at a practice facility, where crowd seating is cramped at best, but the presence of James, the Ohio schoolboy phenom who was the N.B.A.'s first overall draft pick, prompted a switch to the TD Waterhouse Center, where 15,123 showed up in a 17,200-capacity arena.

Season-ticket holders were admitted free, but some 7,000 others paid $5 a ticket. Outside, before the game, there were even instances of ticket scalping, said Joel Glass, the Magic's media director.

"I like playing before big crowds," James said. "I think I play better. As I told some of these guys, my crowds in high school were bigger than some of the Cavs' crowds last year."

Glass said he issued about 175 news media credentials for James's debut. "This is like the playoffs in July," Glass said of the news media interest.

"I've been lifting a lot of weights," James's slender teammate Darius Miles said, smiling. "I'm trying to get my body ready for TV."

Playing point guard tonight despite being 6 foot 8 inches and 240 pounds, James didn't disappoint.

Shortly after being knocked down by the Magic's Alton Ford early in the game, James drove to the basket and missed a 6-foot jumper. But then he quickly stole an outlet pass and dunked.

James was so wound up that he grabbed the ball after the dunk and threw it out of bounds, prompting a delay-of-game warning. No matter. Next, he received a pass inside with his back to the basket, spun and made a 5-footer. Then came a deft pass inside to center DeSagana Diop for an easy score.

James followed that up with another nifty pass, this time to DaJuan Wagner, who missed a layup. On the Cavaliers' next trip down the floor, James found the shot clock winding down and tried a shot from well beyond the 3-point line. It missed everything, sailing out of bounds.

Yet from that humbling moment came his best first-half highlight. Receiving a pass from Miles, James held the ball as his momentum carried him under the basket, then used the backboard to spin in a shot. It drew wild applause from the crowd.

"That's just athleticism," James said. "That's a God-given talent there. I don't know how I did it either."

James provided plenty of evidence as to why he has already evoked memories of a similar-size point guard who is considered among the game's greats. "LeBron is an athletic Magic Johnson," Miles said.

James's early intent as a pro has been to concentrate on his distinguished passing ability, in part to show his teammates that he is willing to share the ball.

Pat Williams, the Magic's senior vice president, said the reaction to James was unprecedented in basketball. The closest to it for a teenager he could recall was when he worked for the Philadelphia 76ers and they drafted Darryl Dawkins out of an Orlando high school in 1975.

The 76ers unveiled Dawkins, a 6-11 player dubbed Chocolate Thunder because of his jarring dunks, in a Philadelphia summer league game. And about 5,000 squeezed into a gym at Temple University, Williams said.

"But there's a special sizzle to this guy," Williams said of James. "He has three attributes that are hard to find in anybody, much less a teenager — maturity, talent and charisma. I think he thrives in the spotlight. In fact I think he would feel uncomfortable if he didn't have it. When you've got those kinds of skills, you want the stage."

James Answers Hype
With Standout Debut

BY CHRIS BROUSSARD | OCT. 30, 2003

SO WHAT IF he was the most touted athlete in the history of high school basketball, or that he is already the best-built swingman in the N.B.A., or that Nike, Sprite and Upper Deck are paying him as if he has equaled the feats of Michael Jordan.

He is still only 18 years old, still only months removed from playing against the likes of Akron Garfield High School.

He will not — cannot — step into the National Basketball Association and excel. No one does that.

They were all saying that before LeBron James's N.B.A. debut Wednesday night.

The experts, the current players, the former stars — all with an I-told-you-so attitude about James's preseason struggles — boldly asserted that it would take time for the prodigy from St. Vincent-St. Mary High School of Akron, Ohio, to electrify the league.

By time they meant games, months, possibly years.

But Wednesday, at ARCO Arena, time was minutes and seconds, as in 1 minute 24 seconds.

With 10:36 left in the first quarter, James boldly introduced himself to his new competition by grabbing a defensive rebound, speeding upcourt with the basketball and tossing an alley-oop pass to his flying teammate Ricky Davis for a dunk.

The play began a first-quarter run by James that, by itself, lived up to the hype of the most anticipated debut in N.B.A. history.

Over the next nine minutes, James, the league's No. 1 overall pick, by the Cleveland Cavaliers, scored 12 points, made 3 steals, gave out 2 more assists and displayed the leaping ability of Jordan and the unselfishness of Magic Johnson.

While James's exploits could not lift the Cavaliers over the powerful Kings, who won, 106-92, they did announce that James's adjustment period in the N.B.A. might last no longer than his college career.

Playing point guard, shooting guard and small forward, James belied his critics by turning in an All-Star line of 25 points, 9 assists, 6 rebounds and 3 steals and shooting 12 for 20 from the field.

Simply put, he was magnificent.

The truest testament to how good James played was the surprising closeness of the game. Playing with a cast that won just 17 games last season, James led the Cavaliers back from a 19-point deficit by recording 7 third-quarter points and 2 assists, the last of which led to a J. R. Bremer 3-pointer that gave the Cavaliers an 85-83 lead.

The buildup for the game was off the charts. The Kings' media relations department issued 340 credentials for the contest, welcoming journalists from England, China, Japan, Germany and Taiwan. The horde followed James as if drawn by hypnosis, surrounding him at the morning shoot-around, at his entrance into the arena, and during his pregame warm-up.

ESPN televised the game and for a few minutes actually cut away from the start of overtime between the Knicks and the Orlando Magic, who feature one of the league's hottest stars in Tracy McGrady, to show the tip-off of James's historic night.

And Moses Malone, the only pro player to demonstrate anything close to dominance in his first year out of high school, was in attendance.

As he has done for the past year, James took the hoopla in stride. But he did admit to being excited.

"It's a dream come true," James said before the game. "I'm afraid to pinch myself because I might wake up. So I'm going to keep living this dream and, hopefully, it don't turn into reality because it seems like a dream right now."

A rude awakening seemed certain, judging from James's first five preseason games. Displaying no touch on his jumper, even lofting a few air balls, he shot about 30 percent from the floor.

But James's last three preseason games gave an indication of what was to come. After Coach Paul Silas switched him to point guard, James averaged 16.3 points, 5 assists and 5 rebounds.

"I just became more aggressive," James said of his surge. "I thought the preseason was good for me, and I'm going to try to keep my aggressiveness and have it carry over into the regular season."

It did just that. Less than two minutes after his first-quarter alley-oop to Davis, James received an entry pass on the right wing, took a dribble toward the baseline and sank his first shot, a 15-foot jumper.

Then he hit one from the left baseline. Then he made a 21-foot fallaway jumper from the right corner over 7-foot Brad Miller. Suddenly, James was dominating, 3 for 3 from the floor.

But he was just warming up. Next, he drove through the Kings' defense for a double-clutch layup, handed out a wicked no-look bounce pass to Carlos Boozer on a three-on-one fast break, and stole the ball at midcourt and finished with a one-handed windmill dunk in which his head was near rim level.

Thirty seconds after his slam, James made another steal and found himself all alone in the paint. But instead of throwing down another dunk, James made an underhand pass to Davis, who was trailing on the play. Davis put in a twisting, highlight-reel slam.

James's most riveting move might have come in the third quarter when he made a winding, left-handed finger-roll layup over Miller in transition. Before the game, Miller had spoken assuredly about not ending up on James's highlight film.

"You've just got to treat him like any other 18-year old," Miller said. "If he drives down the lane and everybody wants to see what he can do dunking-wise, you've just got to give him a hard foul and welcome him to the league right away."

Miller did not know then that James was unlike any other 18-year-old. But he, and the rest of the N.B.A., know now.

LeBron Carnival Makes Its Debut

BY SELENA ROBERTS | OCT. 30, 2003

THE EXECUTIVE CAREGIVERS of the National Basketball Association fret over the immaturity of teenagers who arrive swathed in blue blankets on their doorstep without so much as a college kegger for a life experience, yet they have become playground pushers of LeBron James.

The league's moral monarchs are so concerned about the lifestyle adjustments for prodigies who use prom pictures as a form of ID that they want a 20-year-old age limit, yet the N.B.A. has given the green light to hype LeBron's 18-year-old image in league-related promotions.

"Once you're in, you're in," Commissioner David Stern explained in a recent telephone interview. "If you're a player in the league, you have all the rights and privileges that come with it."

Under the logic of this mixed message, exploitation is simply a form of flattery, a sign of acceptance.

If LeBron's jersey is the hottest merchandise in the store window, if his presence in Cleveland has filled the previously abandoned warehouse known as Gund Arena, if companies are willing to risk $100 million on his potential, why shouldn't the league have grabbed a slice of the kid by launching his N.B.A. debut on national TV last night?

After all, hypocrisy is good for business, particularly when it comes in the shape of a diversion. The moment LeBron planted his new Nikes on the floor against the Sacramento Kings, the instant he provided an initial validation of his talents with his sleight of hand in a 25-point, 9-assist performance, even in a 106-92 loss, he nudged the league's perception problems into the background.

Suddenly, the conversation was not about how Kobe Bryant will play this season with a rape trial looming or how self-absorbed Kobe and Shaquille O'Neal have been to squabble over who's the man while Los Angeles burns or how many players had summer brushes with the law.

Last night, the woes gave way to wonder. "I'm afraid to pinch myself," the very likable LeBron said before tip-off. "I might wake up."

This dream world of LeBron's was, in part, manufactured by ESPN, the Disney Company's underling, from the moment it first broadcast LeBron's high school games last season. Curiously, it was also the first year of ESPN's television deal with the N.B.A.

Not to be too conspiratorial, but it's not so far-fetched to believe that ESPN purposely built LeBron's myth to lay the foundation for ratings growth this season. If there isn't a next Michael Jordan, why not let Disney invent one? (The makers of fairy dust cannot do worse than the league's failed attempt to turn Vince Carter into a Jordan facsimile.)

If ESPN scripted LeBron's intro, the beneficiary of this hype-it-and-they-will-come philosophy is the N.B.A. LeBron was delivered to the league prepackaged. Add water, instant draw.

But does LeBron's prefab fame have an expiration date? If LeBron is a bust, will fans feel hoodwinked? Given the excess of his existence, LeBron has little margin for error, a situation that is worrisome for everyone who understands how fragile the psyche of a teenager can be.

Take Charlie Gibson and Diane Sawyer, the hosts of "Good Morning America" on ABC, another Disney satellite. As they discussed yesterday morning, the crush of pressure on LeBron is unbelievable. With furrowed brow, they expressed heartfelt apprehension about his welfare — right before ABC teased the time for ESPN's coverage of his debut.

Synergy has no room for genuine compassion. There's always a bottom line. The age limit issue has one, too. Stern may well have a teenager's best interests at heart in trying to protect the young from being eaten in the N.B.A., but there is a financial incentive for owners, too.

In the current collective bargaining agreement, there is a five-year rookie salary scale. That means an 18-year-old player is eligible to sign for the heavy-duty maximum money at age 23, followed by another deal before he hits 30.

If a player enters the league at 22, the owners will save money in the long run. There are only so many lucrative contracts in the career of a superstar.

In the N.B.A., an ulterior motive lurks around every corner. Beware, LeBron. The godsend for LeBron's sanity and safety may be Cleveland Coach Paul Silas, known to be soothing amid chaos, a man with a Joe Torre temperament. There are rules — Silas barred LeBron's vast entourage from practice — but there is also guidance counseling.

As a voice of reason, Silas appears to have LeBron's ear.

"He has helped me to maintain and stay focused and kept me away from the things that might destroy me," LeBron said. "Everyone knows the coaching aspects of him, but I like him as a person."

True, Silas's success is tied to LeBron, but amid the carnival, he offers a needed dose of perspective.

"The paraphernalia in the gift shop is all LeBron," said Silas, citing the Cavaliers' store. "We actually had to tell our own people that we had some other guys on the team. The one thing I try not to do is make him different than anybody else.

"Once LeBron sets foot out here, he's got to come with it like everybody else."

Patience is a luxury for Chosen Ones, though. Is it too much for a teenager to handle? Is the answer an age limit, or is it restraint? The same folks who fret over the fragility of teenagers can't help taking a piece of them. The hypocrisy is too tempting.

James's Debut Leaves Critics Gushing

BY CHRIS BROUSSARD | OCT. 31, 2003

IF ANYONE WAS going to bring millions in the basketball world back to reality, back from premature visions of an 18-year-old playing like an N.B.A. superstar, it would be Larry Bird.

After all, Bird, the Indiana Pacers' president, was a longtime rival and buddy of Magic Johnson's, a nemesis to Isiah Thomas and one of the few players to foil the postseason plans of Michael Jordan.

So Bird would certainly put LeBron James's dazzling debut in perspective by reminding us all of the wisdom of the wait-and-see approach, right?

Wrong.

After watching James record 25 points, 9 assists, 6 rebounds and 4 steals in Cleveland's 106-92 loss to Sacramento on Wednesday night, Bird was as smitten with James as everyone else. He has anointed the Cleveland Cavaliers rookie as the truth. Not the truth in a year or so, but right now.

"He's going to be one of the top players in the league by the time the season's over," Bird said yesterday in a telephone conversation. "These other players in the league, these veterans, can say all they want about him not being ready, but this kid is for real.

"I've never seen anybody like this. He passes as well as anybody I've seen, and with his quickness, his size and his strength — I hate to put a label on a guy, but if we're not talking about him being in the Hall of Fame within the next five years, something went wrong. He's the best talent I've seen come out in years."

James did nothing to change Bird's mind in the Cavaliers' 95-86 loss to the Suns here Thursday night, recording 21 points, 12 rebounds and 8 assists in what looked like an almost effortless performance. If there can be any criticism of James after two games, it might be that he has not asserted himself enough offensively. He is so controlled and nonchalant that it seems he can be more dominating if he wants to be.

A check around the league revealed that Bird's sentiments were closer to the rule than the exception.

"People that do this for a living knew," said John Nash, the general manager of the Portland Trail Blazers. "I don't think it sent shock waves throughout the league. I think what we saw against Sacramento will be a consistent performance for him."

James's performance was by far the best N.B.A. debut of any of the current high-school-to-the-pros stars, including Kevin Garnett, Kobe Bryant and Tracy McGrady. The previous record for points scored in a debut by such a player was 10, shared by Jonathan Bender of Indiana in 1999 and Amare Stoudemire of Phoenix last season.

James's 25 surpassed the totals of Garnett (8), Bryant (0), McGrady (0), Jermaine O'Neal (2), Kwame Brown (2), Eddy Curry (2) and Tyson Chandler (1) combined.

Nash believes James will not struggle through an adjustment period like some of his predecessors because at 6-8 and 240 pounds, he already has an N.B.A. body.

"Unlike other youngsters that come into the league that might need an opportunity to develop physically, he's already way ahead of his peers in terms of his physical maturity," Nash said. "He was a man among boys last year, and now he's a man among men. So he's not going to suffer as a result of not being as big as the other guys in the N.B.A. Physically, he's a force."

James was a force in the world of marketing before he hit his first jumper against the Kings. With endorsements from Nike, Sprite and Upper Deck surpassing $100 million, there was a lot riding on James's shoulders Wednesday.

Naturally, Nike, which signed him to a seven-year, $100 million contract, liked what it saw. James wore his Air Zoom Generation sneakers, which will be in stores on Dec. 20.

"We think we have the athlete in LeBron that people want to

emulate," said Rodney Knox, Nike's public relations director for basketball and football.

Rod Thorn, the president and general manager of the Nets, said he was most impressed by James's ability to excel under such pressure at Arco Arena, one of the most raucous gyms in the league, against one of the league's elite teams.

"How about the court presence that he has?" Thorn said in a telephone interview. "Isn't that amazing that he can go out and play as under control and play as well as he played with the hype of that game? It's a special kind of player that would not succumb to that and try to do crazy things to try to live up to the hype."

James grabbed his first rebound and made an alley-oop pass (a dunk by Ricky Davis) within the first two minutes. By the end of the first quarter, he had 12 points, 3 assists, 3 steals and an awe-inspiring dunk.

"Now I can see what all the media is so ecstatic about," Sacramento's Bobby Jackson said after the game. "He's a terrific talent."

James also displayed Magic Johnson-like unselfishness by forgoing a breakaway dunk to pass back to a trailing Davis, who finished with a two-handed reverse slam.

When asked why he passed back to Davis, James said: "That's just me. I'm a team player. He's the scorer. I'm the point guard. That's what point guards do."

Joe Dumars, the Pistons' president, said, "LeBron plays to win and not just for stats."

Cleveland Coach Paul Silas admitted that he did not expect such a start from James. "I knew he was capable of it," Silas said. "I just didn't think it was going to happen. This is a great start for him."

James had come under fire after shooting below 40 percent in the preseason, and rather than gloat after shooting 12 of 20 against the Kings, he joked about his skeptics.

"Coach Silas told me not to start until the regular season," James said with a smile. "I like criticism. It makes me stronger. All those who said I couldn't shoot, thank you. Ya'll helped me a lot."

His debut on ESPN generated a 2.8 rating (or 2.49 million cable households), higher than the rating for all but one of the network's N.B.A. games last season (the first game in which Yao Ming played against Shaquille O'Neal).

Dennis Johnson, Bird's former Celtics teammate and now a scout for Portland, was more cautious about predicting that James would be a dominant force all season.

"We have to keep it all in perspective and perspective says the kid is 18 years old and he's going to stumble," Johnson said. "When he gets to 30 games, he's going to get tired and that's where you may see a little downfall. But with his size and ability, he may catch on again real quick. I hope he does. I hope he's everything everyone writes him to be."

While nothing is promised, 25 points and an endorsement from Bird is a good start.

In Year 1, James Pumped the Volume to 11

BY HARVEY ARATON | APRIL 15, 2004

THE FEW DOZEN STEPS from the court to the Madison Square Garden employee elevator could not be traveled without a handful of jerseys held out, accompanying voices pleading for attention. Even in the sanctuary of a mostly vacant N.B.A. arena, after the late morning shoot-around, celebrity found LeBron James.

"It started crazy but it's actually gotten worse," Cleveland Cavaliers Coach Paul Silas said. He snickered, shook his head and added, "I have so many people I know saying, 'Can you get LeBron to sign this?' "

Silas, an N.B.A. lifer who thought he had seen everything, said that it had been an exhaustive, regular-season haul, and James would later agree.

"A lot thrown on me this year," James said, sounding bored with the repetition of nightly inquisitions and 3 a.m. check-ins.

Three weeks ago, the Cavaliers were rolling toward the playoffs, but the wheels came off and LeBron's rookie revue made its scheduled closing last night, on Broadway, defeating the Knicks, 100-90. The Knicks move on now, with 15 other playoff entrants, to their preferred first-round series against the Nets. James goes home to northern Ohio to work on his jump shot.

The pro basketball season has many weeks remaining and in a definitive sense is only getting started. But if it feels as if the main event for 2003-4 has already happened, that's because this season will ultimately be remembered as James's coming out party.

Even if the argument can be made that he wasn't the league's most successful rookie.

Carmelo Anthony lighted up at least as many nights in the formidable Western Conference, and his team, the Denver Nuggets, made the playoffs. My guess is the voters won't hold James accountable for the Cavaliers' late-season slide, which coincided with an injury to their point guard, Jeff McInnis. Cleveland still stretched its victory total to 35 from 17 and James easily met the soaring expectations for a teenager who last spring had more self-appointed advisers than throwback jerseys.

So many weighed in with the opinion that James should resist turning pro so he might model a college uniform for the financial benefit of a university's athletic department — as opposed to profiting from this season's most popular N.B.A. jersey, based on sales made by the league's Fifth Avenue retail outlet and Web site.

"I never even thought of playing for any of those college teams," James said when asked if he had felt regret last month.

Only during March would anyone question his wisdom. You couldn't miss the self-congratulatory announcers and pundits marking another round of tournament madness by reminding the gifted and talented everywhere not to waste their precious youth in the pursuit of a few million bucks.

Everyone loves the college game, including those determined to avoid it. It is college that so many of the players aren't so enamored of. Billy Packer and Dick Vitale love celebrating the clamor, but what they never talk about is how the band doesn't play and the fans don't cheer on those dreaded Monday morning strolls to class.

If James does edge Anthony in the balloting, it will make two straight years — last season's winner was Amare Stoudemire — that the rookie of the year has gone from high school to elevated N.B.A. proficiency. No wonder there is speculation that more young men than ever will be taken in the first round of the coming N.B.A. draft, and Commissioner David Stern is finally talking about establishing a true minor league.

"You keep hearing like five or seven of the first 10 picks," Silas said. "It's crazy."

For context in determining what's really nuts, how about a 14-year-old being signed to a contract that instantly makes him the

NATHANIEL S. BUTLER/NATIONAL BASKETBALL ASSOCIATION/GETTY IMAGES

LeBron James rests before the game against the New York Knicks at Madison Square Garden last night.

highest-paid player in a professional soccer league? Again, James wasn't buying. "I'm happy for Freddy Adu," he said. "He's a Nike person."

College is a conundrum. Commerce is a calling. Maybe in a few years, Adu will be to D.C. United on the field what James has been to Cleveland on the court and what he promises to be on Madison Avenue for the N.B.A.

There are appealing playoff angles aplenty this spring: Kevin Garnett with a serious posse for the first time; the continuation of the Kobe Bryant story; Tim Duncan's title defense; the growing belief that Indiana or Detroit can mount a challenge to the West. Here in the New York metropolitan area, we now have a four-of-seven-game showdown between Stephon Marbury and Jason Kidd, between the pride of Midtown and the planned migrants to Brooklyn.

The playoffs will have their customary long and winding run, but it's also a good bet that scoring will continue to sag and television viewership will again be flat as the league remains in an existential holding pattern, waiting for its next ratings wave to ride.

Year 1 of LeBron James's career did nothing to dispel the hopes that he will eventually be that vehicle. Fans flocked to his games, grabbed his jersey off racks and, most of all, stood in awe of his skills.

"Longest season I've ever been part of," James said last night.

The next one can't come too soon.

James Is Earning His Wings

BY LIZ ROBBINS | NOV. 21, 2004

CHARLOTTE, N.C., NOV. 18 — LeBron James surged about 10 feet from the basket, grabbed the pass and levitated — the top of the ball nearly level with the top of the backboard. For a moment, he was suspended in the rare air between prodigy and superstar.

And then with one hand he threw down a ferocious dunk, drawing jaw-dropping oohs from the Charlotte fans, lifting the city's mayor out of his sideline seat and leaving the Bobcats' owner, the television mogul Robert L. Johnson, shaking his head.

"I told you all I could fly," James said with a grin after the Cleveland Cavaliers trounced the expansion Bobcats on Thursday night. "I like it up there. Not too many people up there with me."

Eight games into his second N.B.A. season, James, 19, is right about that. By week's end, he was the league's third-leading scorer, averaging 27.4 points, nearly 8 points more a game than last season, and he was averaging six assists and eight rebounds. He helped launch the Cavaliers on a six-game winning streak coming into Madison Square Garden for Sunday night's game against the Knicks.

James, already a $100 million pitchman before suiting up for one playoff game, is rising to the level of his own hype.

He much prefers the hang time he had Thursday night to the one he experienced with the United States Olympic team for 35 agonizing days last summer. The obvious elevation in James's game this season, two years removed from St. Vincent-St. Mary High School in Akron, Ohio, can be traced to his uncomfortable benching in Athens.

"I felt like that was my opportunity to showcase my talent to the world, and I really wasn't provided the opportunity to," James said in an interview Thursday.

"I thought that I was on board to help us win, that's why I was invited, and that's the most disappointing thing. I wasn't there just to be a practice player."

Coach Larry Brown favored the veteran players (with the exception of point guard Dwyane Wade) because of his coaching philosophy, but also because he wanted James to play better defense.

For the first time in his life, James, the reigning rookie of the year, did not start; in eight games, he averaged 5.4 points in 11.4 minutes a game, with 19 field goals and 13 assists. His agent, Aaron Goodwin, flew to Athens to support him. Goodwin recalled his client's fierce declaration one night. "He said he couldn't wait to get back to the N.B.A.," he said.

The United States wound up settling for a bronze medal.

Cavaliers point guard Jeff McInnis said: "He wants to prove to Larry Brown and everybody he belongs and can play. Not only that, he wants to lead our team."

Because of the coverage James demands from defenses, he has opened the floor for center Zydrunas Ilgauskas, who is having an All-Star season. "He makes it so much easier," Ilgauskas said.

When James found McInnis in stride on the fast break and Ilgauskas finished with a clean slam Thursday, James showed more emotion than he had on his highlight-clip dunk.

"That's what I'm talking about!" James screamed.

"If I'm out there 40-something minutes a game, that's what I love to do," he said in a quieter moment. "Playing with the Cavs, I'm back to what I'm used to."

But James is a much different player. His coach, Paul Silas, said, "I've never seen a player from one year to the next change as much as he did."

James already had a chiseled 6-foot-8 body, with an explosive first step and an uncanny instinct for the game. Now, Silas said, he has a more consistent outside shot to go along with his ability to read defenses, pass out of double teams and lead by voice and by will.

"He was like a deer in the headlights last year, and now he just knows what to do," said Silas, who moved James to small forward from shooting guard. "It's the confidence that, 'I want it and I can deliver.' "

Usually that happens when the team needs him most, the hallmark of the great player. In the Cavs' overtime comeback victory against Phoenix on Nov. 10, James scored 17 of his 38 points in the fourth quarter.

He had 33 points and 12 rebounds against Golden State on Monday. Against Charlotte, James scored 18 of his 19 points in the first half, including two 3-pointers and the dunk that punctuated a game-breaking 12-4 run in the final five minutes of the half.

"The game reminded me of when Dr. J first came into the league," Bobcats Coach and General Manager Bernie Bickerstaff said. "He would make plays and everyone would start watching him. It seems that everyone came to watch LeBron, and this is inclusive of us."

James knows he is being watched on and off the court. Last season, the Cavaliers averaged 18,755 fans on the road, second only to the Lakers; the Cavs sold out 33 of 41 road games. His was the top-selling jersey in the N.B.A.

This month, James's new Nike commercial is being broadcast. In it, he is a character in his own video game, "Chamber of Fear," and fights five demons. James worked on the commercial in Los Angeles a couple of weeks after the Olympics in Athens, where he had confronted the demons of criticism and self-doubt.

"That was probably one of the best commercials ever, man," James said, shaking his head. "It's just something to turn LeBron James into a global aspect."

James not only flies like Michael Jordan on the court, but he and his handlers also seem to have grasped the international marketing that helped Jordan single-handedly transform the league.

"I would never put anybody in Michael's category, but LeBron has a potential to be a major driving force in the N.B.A. and outside the N.B.A.," said Johnson, who founded Black Entertainment Television.

Johnson cited James's unselfishness, talent and spotless record off the court, saying, "You got to sit back and say, 'This guy understands what it's all about,' not only for himself as a player, but himself as a professional business person, as an icon and a brand."

But something about James's commercial is telling, said Nova Lanktree of Lanktree Sports, a celebrity marketing group that brokered deals with Jordan.

"It's theatrical," she said. "But do you really get his personality? When Michael smiled and did his thing, his personality was transcendent."

James, polite with an endearing grin, is still guarded, by design. He wants the focus to be on basketball, not on his new life.

This fall, he became a father, and he is rearing his son with the mother, who is from Akron. He said the baby was not keeping him up at night. James was reluctant to share the boy's name, but he did speak about how his son had changed him.

"Just me being more humble," he said. "It's really calmed me down by being a father now. It keeps me real grounded. I got a lot more responsibilities. I got to represent for my whole family now. I can't, in no way shape or form, try to hurt my name."

At times, James acts like the teenager he still is — he turns 20 on Dec. 30 — goofing with McInnis on the bench.

Silas spoke with Brown about James and the Olympics at the preseason coaches meeting. "He talked about him and how far he had to go to be a super player," Silas said. "And I agreed with him."

But then he smiled, grateful for James's source of motivation.

"He came back off the charts," he said.

Skipping Straight to the James Era, With One Caveat

BY HARVEY ARATON | FEB. 20, 2005

DENVER — Carrying bottled water in his hand and the fervent hopes for another N.B.A. renaissance along with Michael Jordan's number on his back, LeBron James nudged through a swelling crowd of journalists here Friday afternoon.

"Let me squeeze through; let me squeeze through," he pleaded, before lowering himself into a chair that Kobe Bryant was kind enough to keep warm.

Consider it just a coincidence of All-Star interview scheduling or a symbolic pecking order of how James, who joined the Cleveland Cavaliers out of high school last season with the hopes of calling Next, has with a stunning swiftness assumed the persona of Now.

Can it be only four years ago that I attended my last N.B.A. All-Star Weekend, in Washington, where a riveting fourth-quarter shootout between Kobe Bryant of the Western Conference and Stephon Marbury and Allen Iverson of the East resulted in Iverson's holding up the most valuable player trophy and Commissioner David Stern's proclaiming the league's future secure in all those sizzling, young hands?

How basketball time flies, and what hops the N.B.A. can flaunt in leaping from one era to another. Marbury, recently self-proclaimed as the best point guard in salaried captivity, didn't even make this All-Star cut. Bryant, 26 (the same number of victories his Shaq-less Lakers have managed thus far this season), said he was just happy to be back in Colorado without his criminal defense team. Iverson, 29, talked about his plans to become a good role model in his dribbling dotage for all the emerging diaper dandies who didn't take Dick Vitale's advice to potty-train in college, starting with the one-named legend known as LeBron.

ANDY CROSS/DENVER POST/GETTY IMAGES

N.B.A. All-Star LeBron James talks to the press before team practice at the N.B.A. Jam Session at the Colorado Convention Center Saturday afternoon.

"That name is going to stand big," Iverson said. "They'll talk about him as being one of the greatest players ever."

What did he mean, will? Sports Illustrated plastered James on its cover last week, wondering if he would be not one of the greatest, but the absolute greatest, and I am assuming this would include that other No. 23.

Speaking of Michael Jordan, have you caught the latest Nike advertisement, in which Spike Lee flips through the six-championship storybook authored by basketball's erstwhile One and Only? In what amounts to a promise that there will be no more comebacks, the commercial concludes by asking, who's next?

It was certainly generous of Team Jordan to acknowledge the possibility of a true successor to His Airness, but it seems the mythmakers in and about the sport have anointed one.

The moral of this story is that you must move fast to keep up with the increasingly and thankfully up-tempo N.B.A., in which the maturation process has been accelerated to the point where James, now 20, can brush off the hype surrounding his first All-Star Game appearance and the skyrocketing expectations.

No big deal, said young James, who is occasionally referred to as King. He's used to the fuss.

"It's been going on for so long, since I was a sophomore in high school," James said.

Jordan has not offered and James has not sought him out for advice on how to deal with the crush of attention, and that's probably a good thing. If James wants to get a handle on his most important challenge — how not to be manipulated into getting ahead of himself — he might want to seek an audience with a fellow starter in tonight's Eastern Conference lineup, Vince Carter, who played a pretty fair Next Jordan until his team in Toronto went south and his body broke down and his reputation crashed.

Or he might corner Kobe to find out how an incredibly talented prodigy who bizarrely adopted many of Jordan's mannerisms and even pulled off a prized three-peat with a little bit of help from Shaquille O'Neal wound up too much in love with himself and ultimately a lone star whose team and Q-score are in free fall.

When James was in high school, he was projected as the next Jordan and Magic Johnson combined. Stylistically and statistically, he has lived up to the billing, averaging 25.3 points, 7.7 assists and 7.2 rebounds, in a league in which no other player totals 25, 6 and 6.

A visionary passer, James devoted himself last summer to improving a suspect jumper and he has, shooting a shade below 49 percent. He has lifted a doormat franchise into solid playoff contention, drawing reactions from peers and coaches that range from utmost respect to outright awe.

"I think he is absolutely unique," said the West coach, San Antonio's Gregg Popovich. "He has all the skills combined: the power, the quickness, the feel for the game. This guy's got the whole package."

Popovich and most everyone whose paycheck is signed by Stern is bullish on the entire cast of young gunners, which is what James, Dwyane Wade, Amare Stoudemire and Carmelo Anthony named themselves at the Olympics last summer.

"A few years ago, there wasn't that great a number of those guys and now there's a lot of them," Popovich said. "I honestly think they are going to be hero-superstars, and it's not about being MTV guys."

Here's the caveat, though, and why the league should proceed slowly, allow these players and especially James to understand that they will be ultimately judged by how they fare in the playoffs, and how serendipity is often as important as their skill sets.

Magic lucked into Kareem. Larry Bird had Robert Parish and Kevin McHale. Jordan didn't win a title until Year 7, when Scottie Pippen began tapping his all-time top-50 talent. We know James — who says he prefers a game-winning assist to a buzzer-beating dunk — passes the ball, but can he share the spotlight? To sit on the throne Kobe once occupied with Shaq, this King may yet have to coexist with an ace.

Remembering King James, Before and After His Crowning

BY HARVEY ARATON | JUNE 16, 2015

BEFORE WE COULD suggest that northeast Ohio was on the verge of its worst depression since the great one of the 1930s, we consulted with Dru Joyce II, who returned from a cruise this week to find LeBron James and what's left of his Cleveland Cavaliers one game away from losing the N.B.A. finals.

It was unfortunate timing, Joyce conceded, a vacation to celebrate an advanced degree in interior design earned by his wife, Carolyn, a mother and grandmother of four.

"We booked it in February and it was all paid for," Joyce said in a telephone interview. "I wanted to shout, 'I'm not getting on that boat unless I know they have TV!' "

He instead sent a text to James to express his remorse about missing Games 3 and 4, last week's return of the finals to Cleveland after an eight-year wait.

James answered, "Enjoy the cruise."

Anyway, Joyce said, he long ago learned to question slavish devotion to a professional sports team, even one carried on the back of James, for whom he has served as a coach and mentor since the basketball prodigy was 10 years old. Art Modell's Cleveland Browns taught him that.

Joyce, the 60-year-old veteran coach of St. Vincent-St. Mary High School in Akron, where the James legend was born, was 9 when the Browns won the city's last major sports championship, in 1964. Years passed. Joyce became a family man, a season-ticket holder, an admitted fanatic.

"I built my life around the Browns, and then Modell picked up and left," he said of the original Browns franchise's move to Baltimore in 1996. "There are other, more important things."

LeBron James, center, with teammates on senior night at St. Vincent-St. Mary's in Akron, Ohio, in 2003.

Perspective is a beautiful thing, especially with the world outside northeast Ohio preparing to marvel at Cleveland's continued sports misery after the Golden State Warriors' 105-97 title-clinching victory Tuesday night in Game 6 at Quicken Loans Arena.

Having played in five straight finals with Miami, in addition to the 2007 sweep at the hands of San Antonio during his first Cavaliers stint, James has now lost four title series in six career tries — the first and last to vastly superior teams. While planning to attend Game 6, Joyce knew what that would mean: more ammunition for the James detractors, and especially those still worshiping at the altar of Michael Jordan.

Jordan was six for six in the finals, and many seem strangely committed to preserving the notion of his singular competitive greatness, as if there were an actual tournament being played across the decades with a winner to be crowned lifetime champion and handed the keys to a fleet of new cars.

They conveniently forget that Bill Russell's Boston Celtics won 11 titles in 13 years. But, O.K., that's ancient N.B.A. news. In modern times, you always got the feeling that Kobe Bryant — No. 24 in your Los Angeles Lakers program, or 23 plus 1 — was in that game. Not so much James, who once suggested that the N.B.A. retire No. 23, made famous by Jordan, and wore Russell's (and Julius Erving's) No. 6 in Miami before reclaiming his old Cavs 23 jersey when he returned this season.

"I honestly believe he's not that caught up in all the other stuff that the media talks about," Joyce said. "He's tried to share with the Cleveland fans from the beginning that winning the title just isn't easy to do. And to be where they are after all that's gone wrong, well, people need to understand that when you've put in the work that he's put in, there's not much more you can ask of yourself."

Legacies need not be limited to the gaudy rings lined with gold, Joyce said. Unlike Jordan, James has used his platform to speak out on perceived social injustice; he has taken on a leading role in the players' union as its vice president; and, even in Miami, he never abandoned his native Akron.

"At this point in his career, Michael was more concerned about selling sneakers," Joyce said. "I know Michael a little, and he might have problems with me saying that. But maybe it was more the people around him, who felt it would be better for his image to just focus on that. LeBron wants to use his platform to do more."

Still, image is not only a subjective concept; in Social Media World, it is hopelessly capricious.

After Game 3, when the Cavaliers held a 2-1 series lead, James all but had his likeness added to Mount Rushmore. After losing Game 5 despite another statistically monstrous game, he said he remained confident because "I'm the best player in the world," and that set off the hater alarms.

News bulletin: James has an ego. As if Jordan — who referred to his teammates, including the great Scottie Pippen, as his supporting cast — did not.

"Look, the Cavs are in a tough situation," Joyce said. "He couldn't be afraid to say that when he is still trying to win this championship, to build on that belief."

James has also said, on multiple occasions during the finals, that he could only do his best and live with the result.

"He's at a place in life where he knows the outcome isn't going to define him in the way he once maybe thought it would," Joyce said. "When he was in high school and getting all that attention, I used to say, 'Do people realize they are hanging on the words of an 18-year-old?' But he's not 18 anymore. He's 30, and he understands that life is bigger than basketball."

James was 10 when Joyce assembled the Amateur Athletic Union team in Akron that included his son, Dru III. For years, he would tell his young wannabes to use basketball as a vehicle, not an ultimate destination.

Dru III just signed for his eighth pro season in Germany, where his wife and two children stay with him, learn the language, soak in the culture and the continent. Another of James's high school teammates, Romeo Travis, has played all over the world.

Talk to the elder Joyce, and you understand that the King's basketball upbringing was no royal, individual showcase, and why he would wake up Wednesday morning, a title dream gone, and know that life is good.

"The kids in Akron will still see him as one of them," Joyce said. "Win or lose doesn't change who he is."

That is the 20-20 view from Northeast Ohio. Can the rest of the world, pitying or pontificating, see it too?

CHAPTER 2

Moves, Basketball and Otherwise

A slew of awards awaited James early in his career. After the Cleveland Cavaliers drafted him in 2003, LeBron James won the Rookie of the Year award. In 2009, James won his first M.V.P. award. James's encounter with major criticism came after his decision to leave the Cleveland Cavaliers for the Miami Heat in 2010. The announcement inspired backlash from his supporters in Cleveland. Yet James won two N.B.A. championship titles with the Heat, and ultimately chose to become a free agent again and return to the Cleveland Cavaliers. In 2016, James succeeded in bringing a championship title to Cleveland.

Cleveland's Venom Validates James's Exit

BY WILLIAM C. RHODEN | JULY 9, 2010

GREENWICH, CONN. — If ever there was a time for LeBron James to leave home, this was it.

The outpouring of venom from the Cavaliers' owner and the wrath of jersey-burning fans betrayed a festering resentment that makes James's decision to leave Cleveland for Miami seem prudent.

This was another extraordinary LeBron moment — first the week-long buildup, then the thousands who gathered here Thursday in front of the Boys & Girls Club to be part of "The Decision." Finally, James, playing "The Bachelor," told us Miami was the lucky franchise.

The most extraordinary part of the event was the reaction of the Cleveland owner Dan Gilbert, who responded on the team's Web site with a venomous, face-saving personal attack that, in its own way, validates James's decision to leave Cleveland.

In an amazing abdication of leadership — and a remarkable revelation of flawed character — Gilbert made James a sympathetic figure.

Referring to a "shameful display of selfishness and betrayal by one of our very own," Gilbert called James's decision process "a several day, narcissistic, self-promotional build-up culminating with the national TV special of his 'decision' unlike anything ever 'witnessed' in the history of sports and probably the history of entertainment."

Yet it was Gilbert who created the King James monster; it was Gilbert who nurtured and reinforced James's prima donna-isms, all of the preening and dancing. Now he acts like a lover scorned and lashes out with gibberish about karma and curses.

Gilbert must think he really owned LeBron James.

Surely, he understands business. You win some, you lose some. With LeBron James, Gilbert won a lot more than he lost. Now, Gilbert has lost a gem in James. And he has lost respect. He has released enough players and let go of enough employees to understand that loyalty, especially in sports, is largely a matter of convenience and timing.

Loyalty is often jettisoned. Look at the hundreds of thousands of Americans who have lost their jobs through layoffs, cutbacks and downsizing.

LeBron got the Cavs before the Cavs could get him.

Will the Heat win a championship? The games still have to be played. This was about power, leverage and options.

James, Dwyane Wade and Chris Bosh built on the Big Three concept engineered by the Boston Celtics three seasons ago when Ray Allen and Kevin Garnett joined Paul Pierce.

What James did throughout the entire process — forcing a parade of billionaire owners to make presentations and brokering a TV special — was an unprecedented act of muscle flexing. This was reminiscent of Muhammad Ali, at least in terms of showmanship. The process was also part Curt Flood, taking the concept of "free" agency to its outermost limit.

With more free-agency cycles to come, N.B.A. owners cannot be happy about this royal production. Clearly, Gilbert isn't. He said "this shocking act of disloyalty from our homegrown 'chosen one' sends the exact opposite lesson of what we would want our children to learn."

On the contrary. There are many lessons contained in the James free-agency drama. The first is controlling the game, not allowing the game to control you.

Here is James, a 25-year-old African-American man with a high school diploma, commanding a global stage.

Adrienne Baytops, the boys basketball coach at the Greenwich Country Day School, was one of the thousands who waited for James here Thursday night. For Baytops, James's actions were not about betrayal or ingratitude.

"This is his job and he's got to make the decision for himself," she said. "The lesson is to stay focused on the big picture, and when you're making a decision, don't get sidetracked by what others think or say or want you to do. He tried for seven years, and it didn't work."

But should a player leave one team for another because he or she wants to win?

Baytops explained that she learned only this week that her star 14-year-old point guard was transferring to a high-profile school in New York City.

"He has an opportunity to go to a dynamic academic school where he'll get more exposure in basketball," she said. "We can't be selfish about these things."

James has chosen. It's Miami against all comers. Now James will be expected to deliver a championship there, or be vilified anew.

Muhammad Ali famously said, "Float like a butterfly; sting like a bee."

He might instead advise James: "Rumble, young man. Rumble."

LeBron James Is a Sack of Melons

BY SAM ANDERSON | JULY 5, 2012

A BRIEF HISTORY OF THE CAREER OF LEBRON JAMES

THERE COMES A TIME in the life span of every culture when it becomes necessary to think obsessively about LeBron James.

The ancient Greeks had to do it in the 5th century B.C., when LeBron James was the most dominant athlete in the Olympic Games. Although he was still just a teenager, he won every event with apparent ease: body grappling, mule tossing, javelin throwing, olive swallowing, stone crushing, bird squashing, neck slapping and running all over the place extremely fast.

And yet he suffered from one inexplicable weakness. As Herodotus tells it in "Histories": "LeBron James — he of the wide forehead and the lumpy shoulders — was a source of much public debate and wonder. His strength and skill were such that his opponents not only lost but they also frequently fled the field weeping bitter tears. Every year, however, when the final and most prestigious event of the Games arrived — the discus throw, in which a victory would have guaranteed LeBron eternal glory — his interest seemed to vanish, like the morning mist, and could not by any means be roused. For no discernible reason, LeBron would slump listlessly to the edge of the field, refusing to throw, sometimes even handing the discus to his friend Demetrus and asking him to throw it in his place. The gods, of course, frowned on such behavior. And so it was that the wrinkliest forehead in all of Greece never felt the touch of the laurel." It is also to this period that most scholars date Plato's famous dialogue "On Clutchness."

Eight hundred years later, LeBron James was the most accomplished gladiator in the entire Roman Empire — this despite the fact that he fought not in the Colosseum but in one of the empire's smaller arenas, very near the town of his birth. Using his trademark gold-tipped trident, he slew bears, lions, elephants, jaguars, ostriches and every variety of man: Moors, Gauls, Huns, Picts, Danes, Angles and Jutes. The legend of LeBron spread rapidly across the empire. Soon he won enough fights to earn his freedom, which gave him the choice to either walk away or to continue fighting, in the arena of his choosing, for what would surely be abundant wealth and fame. The emperor himself lobbied for LeBron James to come fight in Rome, where he would perform in front of the most knowledgeable and passionate gladiator fans in the world.

Finally, after several drama-clogged months, LeBron James announced his intentions. He called a public meeting in the Roman Forum, at the very spot from which Marc Antony had addressed his countrymen after the death of Julius Caesar. (Some found this choice of venue distasteful.) "I have decided," James declared, "to take my tridents to Sicily."

This came as a surprise to many: the gladiatorial scene in Sicily was rather provincial, its arena small and poorly attended. There were, however, other dominant fighters in Sicily with whom James was eager to team — a lion named Jade and a dancing bear named Squash. From then on, they fought exclusively as a trio, doing well sometimes and not so well at other times. Spectators around the empire found this all to be rather anticlimactic. Interest in gladiator fighting dwindled, and many scholars believe it is no coincidence that the sport was officially banned, without public outcry, just a few decades later.

Among the 16th-century Aztecs, LeBron James was the undisputed king of the *ullamaliztli* players. While most competitors specialized in one or two areas of the game — bouncing the ball off their hips or off their knees or throwing themselves to the ground in order to bounce the ball off their spines — James excelled at all of these skills and at many more besides. Once, in Tenochtitlan, at the New Fire ceremony inaugurating the 52-year cycle of the nine Lords of the Night, James bounced the *ullamaliztli* ball through the stone ring so many times that the official scorekeeper ran out of sacred parrot heads with which to keep track.

Afterward, during the postgame fertility festival, James promised the territorial chief that he would win "not one, not two, not three, not four, not five, not six, not seven" *ullamaliztli* championships but (the implication was) many more. The fallout from this statement afflicted Mesoamerica for many years. Some blamed James's boastful statement for the subsequent invasion of the Spanish, the fall of the Aztec Empire, the plague of fire ants in Hispaniola and, eventually, the Deepwater Horizon oil spill.

SOME THOUGHTS ON THE PRESENT

It is now our turn, here in 21st-century America, to think obsessively about LeBron James.

For roughly 10 years, in his current incarnation, LeBron James has been a flying contradiction — a man whose every positive virtue contains its own negation. He is (according to the popular narrative) both lovable and odious, a ball hog and too deferential, incredibly clutch and a choke artist. He is Schrödinger's superstar: simultaneously one of the very greatest players of all time and a fundamentally flawed squanderer of talent. If anything, his championship this year will not simplify this story. It only makes it more complex.

Michael Jordan (to invoke the obvious touchstone) benefited, by comparison, from an impossibly coherent narrative — a story of mythic triumph straight out of Joseph Campbell, in which a naïve young hero passes through the crucible of failure until he finally, triumphantly, rescues the entire culture. (Jordan rescued America from short shorts, the 1980s and Karl Malone.) Jordan's identity, in both existential and basketball terms, was always clear: he was a slender, aggressive, well-rounded, improbably athletic shooting guard who would stop at nothing to eviscerate you and all of your children and all of your children's children. (Kobe Bryant and Dwyane Wade are recognizable iterations of this species.)

James has always been harder to place. On the court, he's a whole anthology of players: an oversize, creative point guard like Magic Johnson; a bodybuilder-style space-displacer like Karl Malone; a harassing, omnipresent defender like Scottie Pippen; a leaping finisher

JARED WICKERHAM/STRINGER/GETTY IMAGES SPORT

LeBron James in the first quarter against the Boston Celtics in Game Three of the Eastern Conference Finals last month.

like Dr. J. He does everything that a human can possibly do on a basketball court; he is 12 different specialists fused, Voltron-style, into a one-man All-Star team.

Somehow this doesn't quite track. Even as we admire James's unique skill set, we're always forced to think about the tension that holds all of the disparate parts together — the contradictory philosophies of the game that all of those different skills imply.

Not to get all physiognomical here, but it strikes me as significant that James is slightly weird-looking. Part of the mystique of Jordan was that he was handsome, beautifully proportioned, graceful — a human so fully aligned with space and time and destiny that his physical shell was just the inevitable outgrowth of a beautiful soul or at least of a beautiful set of skills supported by a beautiful marketing plan.

James is, shall we say, less classically handsome than Jordan — and in a way that perfectly expresses his LeBron-ness. His appearance, if anything, is a little mystifying. Even when he was the most hyped teenager on the planet, there were constant jokes about how he looked like an old man. As he has inched through his mid-20s, bloggers have devoted thousands of words to his apparently receding hairline. If Jordan looked like a walking Michelangelo sculpture, James looks like a sculpture by one of the Mannerist artists from the generation that followed Michelangelo — the ones who piled up lumpy muscles so obsessively that Benvenuto Cellini once compared one of their statues to "a sack of melons." LeBron James is a sack of melons. His face is a theater of strange beards and scowls. In the course of working my way through the vast public discourse online about his appearance, I picked up a new vocabulary word: "uglyphine" — the paradoxical zone of attractiveness where beauty and ugliness merge.

This seems to be the key to James: he is built, as impressively as possible, out of irreconcilable parts. (An ad campaign, for Nike, captured this aspect of his personality: he was a whole clan of people by himself — a family of LeBrons, all in conflict.) Even the two halves of his name pull against each other: "LeBron" has a Francophone echo; "James" is classic Anglo-English.

James's relationship to basketball sometimes seems almost incidental, as if he's less an athlete than a crypto-hulk sent from outer space to problematize our very notions of humanity's relationship to the time-space continuum. It has become a kind of parlor game, among fans, to speculate on how good James would be at other sports: football, say, or track and field. But I'd argue that James has an unusually intimate relationship with basketball — a sport that is itself, as James is, cobbled together out of irreconcilable parts: James Naismith invented it, out of desperation, with a peach basket and a football and the rules of an old children's game called Duck on a Rock.

The result was a particularly American sport in which everyone on the floor is allowed to do everything — unlike football or baseball, in which teams are built out of carefully restricted specialists. Since James can do everything as literally no other player in basketball history could, he plays very close to the core of the game — maybe closer than anyone ever has. In this sense, LeBron James is basketball — the beauty and the problem of the sport embodied. Somehow that makes his relationship to the game much more complicated than anyone else's, and our expectations for him weirder and harder to calibrate.

Now that the planets have at last aligned for James — now that he has his title and excelled in crunch time and silenced pretty much all of his critics — we can finally read him as a coherent sports narrative. His "naive failure" phase has passed; the age of triumph has arrived. This feels simultaneously wrong and right.

WHAT THE FUTURE HOLDS

In the wake of the 36th-century Moon Wars, here in the time beyond time — in which all events exist alongside one another in a perpetual borderless eternity — LeBron James is the unanimous M.V.P. of interplanetary quarkball. His highlights, which recur infinitely, are too numerous to name: there is the match in which he splits 12 of his team's final 13 atoms; the match in which he rides every wave of the light spectrum, visible and invisible, all the way to the event horizon of the neighboring galaxy's black hole; the match in which he executes a spin move so powerful that it opens a parallel world. And yet despite all of these heroics, just because of the nature of quarkball, it is impossible to tell whether James is winning or losing. It has to be assumed, in fact, that he is doing both at the same time, at least until the universe reaches its inevitable trigger point — called by physicists the Decision — at which point the time flow will be born anew and James's fortunes will be resolved, suddenly and irrevocably, one way or the other, toward victory or defeat.

The Decision, physicists say, will manifest itself in one of two forms. If LeBron James is victorious, the moons will disappear, rendering gravity null and dissolving the membrane between life planes, opening the way to a higher consciousness for all beings everywhere.

If he is defeated, the Sun will engulf the Earth.

The Decision Is Reversed, and Cleveland Is in a Forgiving Mood

BY SCOTT CACCIOLA | JULY 11, 2014

FOUR YEARS AFTER he bolted to Miami from Cleveland in pursuit of the N.B.A. championships that had eluded him, LeBron James is returning home.

At age 29 and with two N.B.A. titles now in his possession, James announced Friday that he would rejoin the Cavaliers, for whom he played in the first seven seasons of his storied professional career.

Vilified in Cleveland when he left for the Heat, denounced and mocked by the Cavaliers' owner, James is likely to find that just about all is forgiven, and more, as he embarks on an effort to bring a championship to a city that has not celebrated one in any major sport in 50 years and that, in recent weeks and days, was almost comically looking for any clue at all to divine what James might be thinking.

In the end, everyone found out together when James, who grew up in nearby Akron, Ohio, and is widely regarded as the greatest basketball player of his generation, made the announcement through Sports Illustrated's website. "My relationship with Northeast Ohio is bigger than basketball," he said at one point in an elaborate 952-word statement. "I didn't realize that four years ago. I do now."

In the statement, which he prepared with the sportswriter Lee Jenkins, James compared his time in Miami to going to college — an experience he never had after jumping straight to the N.B.A. from St. Vincent-St. Mary High School in Akron. But now, he wrote, he felt prepared to return and take a responsibility to be a leader, not just on the court but in his home state.

It was all in stark contrast to the way he announced his departure in 2010 — in a televised special on ESPN called "The Decision" that struck many viewers as self-serving, particularly when James stated that he was going to "take my talents to South Beach." And a day later, when he was elaborately welcomed in Miami, he boastfully spoke of how many titles the Heat would now win, saying, "Not two, not three, not four, not five, not six, not seven. ..."

This time, James was far more modest and circumspect. "I'm not promising a championship," he said in Friday's statement, as if to knowingly caution the city of Cleveland to calm down a bit. "I know how hard that is to deliver."

He added: "Of course, I want to win next year, but I'm realistic. It will be a long process."

James's departure from Cleveland in 2010 left deep psychic wounds on the city. On the night of his televised decision, fans burned replicas of his jersey and tossed memorabilia into trash bins. Dan Gilbert, the Cavaliers' owner, posted a vitriolic letter to the city on the team's website in which he referred to James as "our former hero" and described his move to Miami as a "cowardly betrayal." Gilbert also pledged that the Cavaliers would win a championship before James did.

Gilbert, of course, was incorrect. But the letter remained online until early this week, when it was removed. By then, James had secretly met with Gilbert in Miami to clear the air and allow Gilbert to make amends.

In his statement, James described his meeting with Gilbert as "face-to-face, man-to-man."

"We've talked it out," James added. "Everybody makes mistakes. I've made mistakes as well. Who am I to hold a grudge?"

On Twitter on Friday, Gilbert essentially opened his arms to James and said no city was more deserving of a winner than Cleveland. Gilbert also wrote that his 8-year-old son had asked if this meant he could wear his LeBron jersey again. "Yes it does!" Gilbert wrote.

In James's four-year absence, the Cavaliers were one of the league's worst franchises, compiling a 97-215 record without making a single playoff appearance. But the team does feature a young, talented core led by Kyrie Irving, a 22-year-old point guard who recently signed a long-term extension. In his statement, James said he viewed himself as a "mentor" and an "old head" who could help Irving become one of the best players in the league.

James's decision to return to Cleveland — where he is likely to be paid $88 million in a maximum four-year deal — came after a long run of rumors and speculation in which every little detail or oddity became a clue — photographs of James posing with friends from Akron on his Instagram account (that must mean something!), or the convoy of moving vans parked outside his home in Miami (although James always ships his cars to Ohio for the summer).

Then came the owl at the Cleveland Zoo who, alas, predicted that James would return to the Heat. But a clam that was said to have psychic abilities went with the Cavaliers. Meanwhile, commentators on ESPN spent an enormous number of hours attempting to analyze James's decision-making process. But in the end, no one quite expected that James would make his announcement in the manner that he did.

In leaving Miami, and the Heat, James is ending a remarkable four-year partnership with Pat Riley, the Heat's president, and with Dwyane Wade and Chris Bosh, his co-stars on the team. It was Riley who figured out how to team up the three players and fit them within the league-imposed salary cap.

Once he did, it all quickly came together. The Heat went to the N.B.A. finals for four straight seasons and won the championship in two of them (2012 and 2013). And James collected his third and fourth Most Valuable Player awards along the way as he emerged as the league's most unstoppable force, with an almost superhuman blend of speed, strength, skill and savvy.

Still, the past season concluded in sobering fashion for James, with the Heat swatted aside by the San Antonio Spurs in an N.B.A. finals that lasted only five games and exposed the Heat's lack of depth. The series also made it clear that Wade, at 32, was a diminished player on chronically aching legs.

In the wake of the defeat, James opted out of his contract so he could explore free agency. It did not necessarily mean that he was leaving the Heat — he could always re-sign — but it seemed apparent that he wanted to see what sort of personnel moves Riley was capable of making to reshape the roster.

Other teams, meanwhile, got busy clearing financial space so they could potentially accommodate James's salary. He delegated his agent, Rich Paul, to meet with officials from the Cavaliers, the Dallas Mavericks, the Houston Rockets, the Phoenix Suns and the Los Angeles Lakers. The franchises lined up, eager to make their pitch.

But if the process itself felt familiar to 2010, with James entertaining offers from a smorgasbord of suitors, it was ultimately very different this time around.

On Wednesday, James met with Riley for about an hour in Las Vegas, where James was hosting an annual basketball camp for elite high school players. It was a chance for Riley to make his last pitch, to keep everyone together. On Thursday, James flew back to Miami, with Wade joining him on the plane.

It was a symbolic moment for the two players, a chance for them to be teammates one last time, on one final leg across the country. Wade is likely to remain with the Heat, as is Bosh, who, in a surprise, has apparently decided to turn down an $88 million free-agent offer from the Rockets, a deal everyone assumed Bosh would accept if James decided he would no longer be his teammate.

Earlier this week, Riley had also signed two capable veterans — Josh McRoberts and Danny Granger — as part of his effort to persuade James. As a result, Riley is not exactly bereft of talent, but for now, at least, he no longer has a title contender.

None of that is of any concern to Cleveland, which watched Riley steal James away four years ago. On Friday, the city was giddy to win him back.

"I looked at other teams," James said in his statement, "but I wasn't going to leave Miami for anywhere except Cleveland. The more time passed, the more it felt right. This is what makes me happy."

LeBron James Awards Game Balls to Friends and Foes

BY SCOTT CACCIOLA | **JUNE 10, 2016**

CLEVELAND — In hockey, they award the three stars. In soccer, the top performer is named the man of the match. And in the N.B.A. — well, someone often gets a Bronny.

In one of his most audacious feats to date, LeBron James has put himself in charge of more than just the Cleveland Cavaliers' offense as they face the Golden State Warriors in the N.B.A. finals. James has also been giving out game balls — real or imagined — to the series' best players, including his opponents.

"It just comes off the top of my mind," said James, who waits for inspiration to strike and then — boom! — gives away a Bronny. "You know the guys that are deserving of it."

Awarding game balls after big wins and milestones is a tradition in sports. But that job typically belongs to the coach, and he usually sticks with players on his own team.

James cannot help himself. So while he frequently gives Bronnys — and it needs to be noted that the term is ours, not his — to teammates like Richard Jefferson, who received one after the Cavaliers defeated the Warriors on Wednesday night in Game 3, James has also been bestowing theoretical game balls on the Warriors. It might be the first time in the history of sports that an athlete has done so.

So there he was, honoring one of the Warriors after the Cavaliers lost Game 1.

"Obviously," James said at his postgame news conference, "the game ball goes to Shaun Livingston."

It was more of the same after the Cavaliers lost Game 2. James cited the brilliant play of the Warriors' Draymond Green, who did not receive an actual game ball from James. But James wanted to make clear that Green deserved one.

"Game ball to him," James said.

Friend? Foe? Makes no difference to James, the Oprah Winfrey of game balls: *Bronnys for everyone!* Everyone, that is, except himself.

For teammates, the game-ball experience can be both bonding ritual and confidence builder. If James, a four-time most valuable player, is taking the time to single you out, it must mean that you did something right. It can have even more of an effect if the team has been struggling.

"When everybody's sort of down and we need a boost and a certain guy lifts us up, I think LeBron's just good at acknowledging it," said the reserve guard Iman Shumpert, who passes along his LeBronified game balls to his mother for safekeeping. "I mean, I would never remember to go grab the game ball. That's why he's LeBron."

James tends to pick his spots. He does not bequeath Bronnys willy-nilly. It has to be an important moment. In January, for example, James gave the game ball to Tyronn Lue after Lue won his first game as the Cavaliers' coach. Teammates and members of the coaching staff never know when James will show up in the locker room with a souvenir.

"Just out of nowhere, he'll bring it in before we break," the assistant coach James Posey said. " 'Game ball goes to so-and-so!' And everyone's like, 'Oh, O.K.!' "

Game balls in general mean more to some players than others. Posey, for example, has kept just one from his long and productive player career — a ball that his teammates with the Boston Celtics gave him after his daughter, Sai, was born in 2008.

James Jones, a reserve guard on the Cavaliers, said the only ball that still had much significance to him was from the game when he scored his first N.B.A. points. He keeps it in a case at his home. Jones has received plenty of other game balls over the years, he said, but their whereabouts are mostly unknown.

"Some of them are probably out in the yard where my kids play," he said.

Keith Dambrot, who coached James at St. Vincent-St. Mary High School in Akron, Ohio, suspects that James's affinity for game balls is a holdover from his days playing football as a teenager. Dambrot, who now coaches the men's basketball team at the University of Akron, said that James did not learn the practice from him.

"We didn't have enough basketballs to give away back then," Dambrot said in a telephone interview.

At the same time, Dambrot said, James was a charitable teammate who could sense the pulse of the team. St. Vincent-St. Mary was involved in its share of lopsided games, but James often acted as a pass-first facilitator. James knew that he needed a supporting cast in order to succeed.

"That hasn't changed," Dambrot said. "He has a knack for understanding his teammates and how to motivate them."

James seemed to be delivering one such dose of inspiration after the Cavaliers won the opening game of their Eastern Conference semifinal series with the Toronto Raptors last month.

"The game ball definitely goes to our bench tonight," he said at his postgame news conference.

As for his bequeathing Bronnys to opponents, James seems to respect good basketball — and possesses the sort of outsize self-assurance required to make such declarations. If there is an ulterior motive, he has kept it to himself.

In any case, the Warriors appear to be less sentimental about keepsakes than the Cavaliers. When the Warriors won their 73rd game of the regular season to set an N.B.A. record, Green made sure to track down the ball, a treasure that could not have foreseen its sad fate.

"We're going to cut it up," Green said, "and give everybody a piece."

Cavaliers Defeat Warriors to Win Their First N.B.A. Title

BY SCOTT CACCIOLA | JUNE 19, 2016

OAKLAND, CALIF. — Vilified when he left and celebrated when he returned, LeBron James had spent the past two seasons lugging his city's championship dreams like a bag of rocks. The weight had only grown more cumbersome — the weight of history, of disappointment, of missed opportunities.

James could feel it all on his sturdy shoulders.

On Sunday night, before a dazed and defeated crowd at Oracle Arena, James delivered on the grandest stage of his superhuman career, leading the Cleveland Cavaliers to their first championship in franchise history with a 93-89 victory over the Golden State Warriors in Game 7 of the N.B.A. finals.

"I came back for a reason," James said. "I came back to bring a championship to our city."

James collected 27 points, 11 rebounds and 11 assists to punctuate one of the most remarkable individual performances in finals history. James, who was named the finals' most valuable player, got ample help from his teammate Kyrie Irving, whose 3-pointer with 53 seconds remaining gave the Cavaliers the lead — and an improbable title.

Improbable because the Cavaliers became the first team to rally from a 3-1 series deficit to win a championship. Improbable because the Warriors, after setting an N.B.A. record with 73 victories in the regular season, had spent months making the case that they were the most dominant team since Dr. James Naismith first affixed a peach basket to a wall.

And improbable, above all, because of Cleveland's ragtag history as an also-ran. Not since 1964, when the Browns won the N.F.L. championship, had the city claimed a major sports title.

James, who grew up in nearby Akron, has forever changed all of that. He stuffed the series with thunderous dunks and fadeaway jumpers, blocked shots and glowering expressions, towing his teammates along in his ferocious wake. James won two championships with the Miami Heat, but this was his first with the Cavaliers — and his first for Ohio.

Not even the Warriors, who were pursuing back-to-back championships in a repeat of last year's finals matchup, could slow his march.

"The game always gives back to people that are true to the game," James said. "I've watched it. I know the history of the game, and I was just calm. I was calm."

Irving finished with 26 points for the Cavaliers, who survived three elimination games. In Cleveland, fans jammed the streets around Quicken Loans Arena for a watch party from afar.

Draymond Green had 32 points, 15 rebounds and 9 assists for the Warriors, and Stephen Curry scored 17 points but shot just 6 of 19 from the field. In the final minute, Curry missed a 3-point attempt that would have tied the game. James, who had made a soaring block of Andre Iguodala's layup attempt with less than two minutes to play, then made 1 of 2 free throws with 10.6 seconds left to seal the win.

The Cavaliers formed a raucous mob at the buzzer — joy and disbelief, all at once. On the postgame dais, James clutched the championship trophy to his chest and choked back tears. At his news conference, he wore one of the nets around his neck. He said he was looking forward to the victory parade, scheduled for Wednesday. He invited everyone, including the media.

"It's going to be the biggest party that Cleveland has ever seen," said James, who averaged 29.7 points, 11.3 rebounds and 8.9 assists during the series. "If you guys still have a little money left over in your budget, you guys better make a trip to Cleveland and get a little piece of it."

From the moment the Warriors set about stalking the 1995-96 Chicago Bulls for the best regular-season record in league history, they cautioned that it would mean almost nothing without a championship, too. The Warriors were greedy — they wanted all the records, all the wins and another trophy at the end.

"We're stunned," Coach Steve Kerr said. "We thought we were going to win."

The Warriors found their postseason journey to be more jagged than they imagined. The tenor of the team's chase was jarred off course in the first game of the playoffs, when Curry injured his right ankle. Three games later, he slipped on a wet spot against the Houston Rockets, spraining his right knee.

Though Curry eventually returned to help guide the Warriors back to the finals, thanks in part to a dramatic comeback against the Oklahoma City Thunder in the Western Conference finals, Curry lacked his usual consistency. More trouble brewed against the Cavaliers.

Green had to watch Game 5 from a baseball stadium after he was suspended for collecting too many flagrant fouls. Andrew Bogut, their starting center, injured his knee and missed the final two games of the series. Iguodala, James's primary defender, tweaked his back in Game 6.

As for Curry, his finals experience was an obstacle course of long-limbed defenders (he shot 40.3 percent from the field), spats with officials (he chucked his mouth guard after he was ejected from Game 6) and volleys from critics, who took jabs at everything from his poor shooting to his choice of sneakers. Game 7 was another slog.

"It will haunt me for a while," Curry said, "because it means a lot to me to try to lead my team and do what I need to do on the court and the big stages. Done it before. Didn't do it tonight."

The Cavaliers were no strangers to adversity. Sensing what he described as dysfunction, General Manager David Griffin fired the team's head coach, David Blatt, midway through the season and replaced him with Tyronn Lue, one of Blatt's assistants. Griffin made the move even though the Cavaliers were sitting firmly atop the Eastern Conference standings.

It was championship or bust for these Cavaliers, who, make no mistake, were formed in James's shadow. Not that his journey was without its share of hard feelings and trapdoors.

Drafted by the Cavaliers in 2003, James splashily left for the Heat as a free agent in 2010. Fans who felt scorned by his departure burned replicas of his jersey in the streets of Cleveland. But James rejoined with the Cavaliers in 2014, vowing to lift the franchise to new heights, to do something that had never been done.

"I don't think people imagined it this way — the route that we've taken — and that's fine," James said Saturday. "Like I always say, every day is not a bed of roses, and you have to figure out how to get away from the thorns and the things of that nature to make the sunshine."

Nobody seemed consumed by the pressure. Kerr arrived at the arena following his usual game-day session of hot yoga with Luke Walton, one of his assistants.

The crowd stood from the opening minutes. After James batted an attempted layup by Curry into an expensive row of courtside seats, Curry got in James's face. An official had to separate them. Green, meanwhile, went 5 of 5 from 3-point range and scored 22 points to guide the Warriors to a 49-42 halftime lead.

The Cavaliers rallied in the third quarter. After Curry committed a turnover, Irving raced away for an acrobatic layup, drawing a foul for good measure. His free throw gave the Cavaliers a 5-point lead. A small subset of fans at Oracle started chanting, "Let's go, Cavs!"

But neither team could find any separation, at least not until James and Irving emerged in the closing moments — not until it mattered most.

The Arc of the LeBron James Story Reaches Its Climax

ESSAY | BY MARC TRACY | JUNE 21, 2016

JAMES PHELAN, A literary scholar at Ohio State, heard it on sports-talk radio on Tuesday, even if fans and hosts weren't saying it outright. The nature of the discussion about LeBron James conveyed that no matter what happened next, after he led the Cavaliers to their first N.B.A. championship Sunday night, his legacy had been definitively chiseled.

There was "implicit recognition that narrative culmination has already occurred," Phelan said. James's career, as inadvertently reflected by the radio banter, was now the stuff of bildungsroman. Right, sports fans? Bear with me.

The hero chafes at the comfort he knows, so he leaves home, believing adventure will give him both spiritual fulfillment and a livelihood. He gains knowledge but comes to realize something is missing. He stumbles back home, where he realizes the key to happiness was right under his nose all along.

It is the plot of the coming-of-age story, grist for dozens of classic 19th-century novels (and yet more middling 20th-century movies).

If even those without Cleveland connections found themselves feeling warm and glad when they watched James drop to the floor at Oracle Arena on Sunday night and weep with joy, it might have been because the arc of his endlessly scrutinized career resembles a tried-and-true story, and this was its completion.

The technical term for a novel of growth is "bildungsroman," a German word (roughly, "novel of development") for a genre that started with a German book. That book — "Wilhelm Meister's Apprenticeship," by Johann Wolfgang von Goethe — describes a well-to-do young man who leaves home and falls in with a troupe of actors, has adventures and finally realizes his destiny lies with a society of the well-to-do that is intimately connected to his origins.

In other words: There's no place like home.

Throughout his sentimental education, to borrow the title of one of those novels, James has satisfied each of its conventions as if he were checking items off a grocery list.

He grew up in Akron, Ohio, near Cleveland. In the early stage of his career with the Cavaliers, when a Nike billboard in downtown Cleveland declared, "We Are All Witnesses," his incredible gifts and the opportunity to write a storybook ending left him feeling pressured and stifled.

In 2010, James beat a path for Miami — trailed by burning jerseys, a nasty letter by the owner Dan Gilbert of the Cavaliers, and a book labeling him "The Whore of Akron" — and won two N.B.A. titles with the Heat.

"Without the experiences I had there, I wouldn't be able to do what I'm doing today," James wrote in a Sports Illustrated essay upon his return to Cleveland in 2014, confirming the necessity of the Miami part of the tale.

But James clarified that merely returning did not close the loop. "What's most important for me," he wrote, "is bringing one trophy back to Northeast Ohio."

As with every other stage of James's career, this was achieved as dramatically as possible. On Sunday night, that vintage chase-down block was reminiscent of his still-present, scampering youth. His brilliant game control — a teammate, Kyrie Irving, compared him to Beethoven composing a symphony — was the signature of so much experience.

Like the hero at the close of every novel of growth, James completely fulfilled society's expectations as well as his own. No matter what comes next, he will never again have a moment as charged with meaning. That part of his life is over.

It is sublime. It is also bittersweet.

"They've found their place in society," Joseph Slaughter, an English professor at Columbia, said, referring to the heroes of such stories.

"It reaffirms natural ideas of home and society," he added, "that everybody will find their place."

The genre, Slaughter said, frequently featured a fatherless man (it was the 1800s, and an autonomous place in society was largely unavailable to women). In "Great Expectations," Pip searches for the father figure who provided him with his inheritance. Huckleberry Finn flees his drunken father and heads for the Mississippi River. And the stories conclude, Slaughter said, when the hero accepts his lot in society. Wilhelm learns he has a son.

James, as those familiar with his story will recall, was raised by a single mother in Akron, finding father figures in basketball gyms and siblings in his teammates, to whom he always preferred to pass the ball and whom he always kept close. After Sunday night's game, James reportedly insisted on three portraits: one with his mother, Gloria; one with his coterie of close friends, some of whom he has known since childhood; and one with his wife and their three children — on Father's Day.

This is real life, of course, and there are complications to James's neat narrative of bildung, or self-formation. In 2010, James saw that the Heat provided the quickest route to a then-elusive N.B.A. championship. Later, he saw promise in Irving and the Cavaliers.

But if we are at times guilty of projecting these narratives onto James's career, this was the natural result of his unmatched collection of basketball talents — bullet speed, freight-train size and beautiful mind — and the knowledge that they would not all last.

James has demonstrated that perhaps no vocation lends itself to the coming-of-age yarn better than athlete. The stark lines of sports provide a clearer focus for the universal fact these stories dramatize: that physical ability unavoidably wanes, infinitely magnifying the pressure to achieve one's goals in a relatively short window of time, which shuts while one is still young.

James could still win another championship or three. He could play for the Knicks, although he probably won't. He could clinch an N.B.A.

finals on Cleveland's home court. He could lead the Cavaliers to a rubber-match series against the Warriors a year from now.

But what he cannot do again is play quite as poignant a role, in his life or in ours. Having won one for Northeast Ohio, he is now the fully formed person he will be for the rest of his life.

"If he wins more, it's denouement; it's not climax," Phelan said. "It's epilogue or sequel."

The bildungsroman, Slaughter said, is "also about the beginnings of middle age — finding that place where you're comfortable, not excited by the same youthful fantasies."

For this reason, Slaughter said, with stunning frequency the bildungsroman ends with the hero between 30 and 33. James is 31.

For someone to find his place so completely, in such triumph, is a wonderful thing. And for the rest of us, it is no small consolation to be able to say that we were all witnesses.

LeBron James Delivered on His Promise in 2016

BY CHRISTOPHER CLAREY | DEC. 22, 2016

LEBRON JAMES WAS present at two Game 7 thrillers in 2016 but played in only one of them.

It was on the night of June 19 at Oracle Arena in Oakland, Calif., where James and the Cleveland Cavaliers faced the Golden State Warriors in Game 7 of the N.B.A. Finals.

Before bringing the trophy home to Ohio — as promised — James and his teammates had to find a way to win on the road, just as they had in the first three rounds of the playoffs.

History was against them. No team had rallied from a 1-3 deficit in the Finals to win the N.B.A. title. And the Cavaliers, founded in 1970, had never won the title, not even when James — the greatest basketball talent of his generation — first led them to the Finals against the San Antonio Spurs in 2007, when he could jump a little higher, recover a little faster and dominate with more margin for error.

But this time James, at 31, was part star, part missionary, and what elevated this into the game of the year from an international perspective was James's drawing power and his throwback sense of community.

There was a glut of transcendent games in 2016: Portugal's first major title at the Euro, secured in extra time in France; Brazil's cathartic grudge match in Rio with Germany that secured its first men's soccer gold medal; the Cubs' curse-terminating victory in the Game 7 that James would attend as a spectator just four and a half months after the N.B.A. finals while wearing a T-shirt that read "Cleveland or Nowhere."

But in a thoroughly mercantile, increasingly globalized sports world, players are still the sum of their actions, and James — who returned from Miami to Cleveland in 2014 — was not only honoring his roots with his old-school loyalty and hunger-pang hustle, he was honoring others' roots, too.

"Look, the city of Cleveland needed this," said Tony Godsick, the Cleveland-based agent who has long represented Roger Federer. "It's been the butt of so many jokes for so long, all unnecessary to be honest. A lot of the things people make fun of were years ago. But LeBron was able — and he was not alone with that great supporting cast — to find a way to change the direction of the series and probably a lot more.

"Harvard Business School can do a study in a few years and really delve into the economic and psychological impact of that win, what it did to a city and a region."

The Cavs' Game 7 was a fine spectacle even without the backstory — 20 lead changes in total; players succumbing or rising to the big occasion.

Cleveland led by 1 when the first quarter ended; the Warriors by 7 at halftime when the Cavaliers coach, Tyronn Lue, made it clear in front of his team that James needed to be a bigger presence.

James was not amused: not after scoring 41 points in Game 5 and 41 more in Game 6. Not after all the team-building and load-carrying he had embraced throughout the season and the series.

"I didn't really think he was playing that bad," Lue later told Sports Illustrated. "But I used to work for Doc Rivers in Boston, and he told me, 'I never want to go into a Game 7 when the best player is on the other team.' We had the best player. We needed him to be his best."

But what was so telling about how much this particular Game 7 meant was that none of the main men were truly at their best down the stretch. Even James forced and missed too many shots in the fourth quarter, but with the score tied at 89-89 with four and a half minutes to play, Golden State went even colder.

The Warriors — the offensive juggernaut that dominated the regular season with a record of 73 victories — failed to score so much as a point the rest of the way.

That was a reflection of Stephen Curry's dip in form and confidence in the playoffs; a testimony to the nerves that a Game 7 can jangle. But it was also a tribute to the Cavaliers' defense and above all to what James did with 1:51 to play.

With the Warriors on a fast break and Andre Iguodala heading for what looked very much like a routine layup, James altered that reality by swooping in from behind, touching the ball an instant before it hit the backboard — an instant before James would have been called for goaltending.

"The Block" will not soon be forgotten, and the other play of the game soon followed when Kyrie Irving broke the tie for good with a 3-pointer over Curry with 55 seconds left.

On Cleveland's next possession, James was fouled on an attempted dunk and fell hard, wincing and clutching his right wrist on his shooting hand as he writhed on the floor. It looked bad, bad enough to make you wonder whether James had now given all he had to give to this phenomenal series and phenomenal game.

But that was selling him and the moment short, and he was soon back on his feet and back at the free throw line, where he went 1-for-2 to give the Cavaliers — and his city — the 4-point cushion they needed.

LeBron James Celebrates 30,000th Point and Then He Scores It

BY BENJAMIN HOFFMAN | JAN. 23, 2018

LEBRON JAMES HAS often pointed out that he enjoys spreading the ball around as much as he enjoys scoring. But as he sat just 7 points short of 30,000 for his career leading into Tuesday night's game against the San Antonio Spurs, the notoriously unselfish superstar threw an online alley-oop to himself off the backboard.

"Wanna be one of the first to congratulate you on this accomplishment/achievement tonight that you'll reach!" James wrote in an Instagram post that featured a photo from his high school days. "Only a handful has reach/seen it too and while I know it's never been a goal of yours from the beginning try (please try) to take a moment for yourself on how you've done it!"

The post went up more than seven hours before James's Cleveland Cavaliers tipped off against the Spurs in San Antonio, but he had good reason to be confident: He had been held to fewer than 7 points just three times in his career, and the last time came on Dec. 29, 2004 when he was 19 years old.

Sure enough, with 1 second left in the first quarter, he sank a 19-footer, giving him 8 points in the game and pushing him to 30,001 in his career. He finished the game — a 114-102 loss — with 28 points, leaving him with 30,021, or 8,366 short of Kareem Abdul-Jabbar's N.B.A. record.

Talking to reporters after the game, Dwyane Wade, who won two N.B.A. championships with James in Miami before joining him in Cleveland, said he was happy he could be on the court for his friend's achievement.

"He can start moving to 35 now," Wade joked. "I'm sure he'll be there in no time."

James joined Abdul-Jabbar, Karl Malone, Kobe Bryant, Michael Jordan, Wilt Chamberlain and Dirk Nowitzki as the only N.B.A. players to reach 30,000. And at 33 years and 24 days old, he shattered Bryant's record for getting to the milestone fastest, as Bryant was 34 years and 104 days old when he hit the mark in 2012. Even accounting for James's status as a prep-to-pro player, allowing him to join the league at an age three to four years younger than that of all the players on the list besides Bryant, James did it in the fourth-fewest games, trailing only Abdul-Jabbar, Jordan and Chamberlain.

Speculation has been rampant over whether James is capable of finishing as the top-scoring player in N.B.A. history — Abdul-Jabbar, with 38,387 points, has been the career scoring leader since he passed Chamberlain on April 5, 1984 — but James has made a point of telling anyone who will listen that he still does not view himself as a scorer, regardless of his career average of 27.1 points a game.

"When you categorize who I am as a basketball player, it won't say 'scorer,' " he told reporters after scoring 16 points in a win over the Orlando Magic last week. "There's too much more attributes to my game, and then you can talk about scoring as well."

James, as he often is, was being too modest. He has 5,846 more points than Abdul-Jabbar had at the same age and he has not averaged fewer than 25.3 points a game in a season since his rookie year.

Making up the gap between him and Abdul-Jabbar, though, will be a challenge. Excluding Nowitzki, who is still active, the five players ahead of James on the scoring list averaged 7,395 points from the season in which they were 34 years old — Basketball-Reference uses a player's age on Feb. 1 as their official age for that season — until their retirement. Chamberlain, who retired at 36, scored the fewest points from his age-34 season forward, with 3,993, while Abdul-Jabbar scored the most with 12,117.

Nowitzki, whose 30,837 career points put him one spot ahead of James on the career list, acknowledged James's achievement on Twitter, as did Bryant.

Congrats @KingJames. Welcome to the club!!!

— Dirk Nowitzki (@swish41) Jan. 23, 2018

From #Akron to #30k @KingJames well done my brotha

— Kobe Bryant (@kobebryant) Jan. 23, 2018

But before James, or Nowitzki for that matter, starts projecting their career too far forward, they would be wise to remember that Bryant proved the end of a career can come far faster than anyone expects. Bryant was still near the top of his game during his age-34 season, averaging 27.3 points a game in a whopping 3,013 minutes. A series of injuries would limit him to 107 combined games over his final three seasons, with his scoring average dropping to 18.9 points a game.

Barring a catastrophic injury, James, who has endured a post-season and international workload during his career that only Tim Duncan would understand, does not see the end as being near.

"Right now, I feel great," he told reporters earlier this month. "I don't feel 33."

He also showed he has not lost his sense of humor, even amid a great deal of turmoil for the Cavaliers this season, pointing out that he has another reason to stick around.

"I've got too many sneakers to sell, still," he said.

LeBron James Delivered.
Now Does He Exit?

BY MICHAEL POWELL | JUNE 7, 2018

CLEVELAND — For four years now, LeBron James has faced brutal June math.

If the man from Akron fails to go galactic in even a single game, if he misses those fallaway jumpers that make defenders close their eyes and shake their heads, if he fails to barrel to the hoop like a B.&O. freight train, if he has trouble levitating to swat away shots, if he is merely human, the Cleveland Cavaliers lose.

Ever since Ohio's native son wandered back from his Miami Beach idyll in 2014, he has, in the N.B.A. championship round, faced the Golden State Warriors, a team that gets more talented each year. James has dragged the weakest Cavaliers team yet to this year's showdown with the Warriors, and now it is perched at the edge of defeat's abyss, down three games to none.

His fans, which is to say a generous portion of the population of Ohio, have a sense of time fleeting.

James will become a free agent, and in his 34th summer, he could well leave for a better-crafted team in another city. Rumors have him going to Los Angeles, Houston, Philadelphia or San Antonio. In 2010, when he left for the Miami Heat, the citizens of Ohio erupted in a collective and pained tantrum, as fans burned his No. 23 jersey and the team's billionaire owner indulged in inane talk of treachery and betrayal.

A replay is difficult to imagine. No doubt some fans will grumble and moan, but he has delivered on his promises. James brought that first championship to Cleveland. It's an intriguing moment when a man and his fans appeared to have matured in their relationship with each other.

Before Game 3 of the N.B.A. finals, I wandered the streets and canal walkways of Akron — Rubber City, baby. Then I headed to Cleveland. And again and again, I heard the same sentiment.

James is approaching late middle age in basketball terms. Through a partnership between his foundation and University of Akron, he showered tens of millions of dollars on college scholarships for poor and working-class kids and he speaks up to a president intent on stirring racial embers to no good end.

A man-child has become a man.

"LeBron? I'll talk LeBron all day long!"

Rachel Walker stops to talk with me in a parking lot within sight of the Cavaliers' arena in Cleveland. She's a nurse and she is taking her adult daughter, who is disabled and wearing a Cavaliers hat, to the game.

"He said he would give us a championship — and he did," she said. "He said he would not forget our children — and he never did. You know why the president doesn't go after the N.B.A.? Because LeBron James will go back at him.

ANDREW SPEAR FOR THE NEW YORK TIMES

A LeBron James mural on the side of a building in his hometown of Akron.

"Whatever he does, I wish him nothing but the best."

I cross the street and sit awhile with Terry Smith, a husky and retired veteran of the railroads. He brought his grandchildren downtown to soak up the pregame vibe. "He brought Cleveland a championship, right? He has tremendous scholarship programs for Akron and Cleveland, right? He plays 48 minutes a game, right?"

Almost: James played 46 minutes 52 seconds in Game 3, four minutes more than any other player.

Having added up the tab, he gives me the total: "He has the right to take care of his family and go wherever he wants."

The Cavaliers and their owner, Dan Gilbert, have not exactly held up their side. The five best players on the court Wednesday evening were James, Kevin Durant, Stephen Curry, Klay Thompson and Draymond Green.

Save for James, all were Warriors.

James could not find the mortar range on his jump shot on Wednes-

Rich Siebert wore a gold sequined jacket with a LeBron James patch to Wednesday's game.

day, but he scored 33 points on a variety of drives, flips, hooks and baby jumpers. He also grabbed 10 rebounds, added 11 assists, had a couple of steals and swatted two more away.

A play in the third quarter was emblematic.

The Warriors' Andre Iguodala, a classy defender and crafty scorer, got the ball near the Cavaliers' hoop. Only James stood in his way. Iguodala faked and faked again. James did not bite, so Iguodala pitched quickly to Green, whose brilliance as a player is diminished only by his adolescent temperament. Green broke into a smile as he rose to dunk, even as James flicked rattlesnake quick hands and slapped the ball off Green's knee and out of bounds.

James immediately took the ball out, came steaming upcourt and tossed a brilliant pass for an assist.

It was like watching a pirate captain swinging from the mizzenmast, dueling all comers: It was great drama, and it works against almost any team not named the Golden State Warriors.

A sign left behind in the arena after Cleveland lost Game 3.

Cleveland's defense, most often a porous swamp, was watertight for much of this night. It held the Warriors' sharpshooting backcourt, Thompson and Curry, to 21 points on 7-for-27 shooting.

Unfortunately, this did not account for Durant. He is seven feet, with elegantly long arms and the soft hands of a jeweler. To watch his pregame workout was its own treat. This night, he stood 20 feet from the basket and had a coach zip him a pass. He caught it and spun 360 degrees on his heel, came to a stop and just as quickly spun back. He immediately shot the ball.

I watched him do this 15 times in a row, and he did not miss once. I looked around for a security guard. Someone needed to pass a note of warning to James.

"He's an assassin," James said afterward.

And here's where the impossibility of this team comes to bear: On any given night, when Curry is shimmying and shooting and Thompson is his metronomic shooting self, Durant is the team's third option.

Nails from a makeshift basketball hoop remain on James's old block in Akron.

Coach Steve Kerr acknowledged the glory of it. "Yeah, it's pretty nice; a luxury," he said.

"You know that you can never, ever relax," James said.

Earlier that day, I sat on George Kimbrough's porch in Akron, and listened as the disabled 71-year-old welder talked of how LeBron purchased hundreds of bikes for neighborhood kids and then led summer rides around his hometown, the Pied Piper of Akron. "That man has earned the right to go and find a team worthy of his talent," Kimbrough said, then looked at me and cackled. "Don't talk bad about that man around here unless you want a fight."

I wander down one ravine to another until I reach Overlook Terrace. It is a dead-end street and there are thickets of beech, black cherry and red oak on three sides. The street has four dowager homes, several well into their dotage. Twenty-five years ago, James and his mother washed up here, after losing one apartment or another. An older woman, Mrs. Reeves, gave shelter from the storm. James quickly put up a poster of Michael Jordan over his bed.

Then he and the neighborhood kids nailed a hoop and wooden backboard to a slanting telephone pole and played all day long. A few twisted nails are still visible. Ben Brown lived there then and now, and he recalls James as a friendly little kid — he holds his hand about three feet off the ground.

Brown has a carpet business, Barefoot Carpet, and ducks and chickens and a tomato patch out back. He figures James long ago earned the right to do as he wants. Maybe he stays, maybe he goes. That's up to him.

We chat for a while longer, and he talks of the college scholarships for local children. He also enjoys that a kid from Overlook Terrace does not back down from an orange-haired provocateur president.

A train whistle sounds loud and mournful. It's the Cuyahoga Valley line rumbling through, just behind those oaks.

"I'm happy for him," Ben says. "James inspires me still."

The N.B.A. Has the Hottest Stove. LeBron James Is the Flame.

BY MARC STEIN | JUNE 30, 2018

LEBRON JAMES IS about to switch teams for the third time in his career. Or he will soon pledge to stay with his home-state Cleveland Cavaliers.

Either outcome will be as noisy as it gets for the social media masses clamoring for N.B.A. player movement — as evidenced by the Twitter hysteria James ignited Saturday by flying with family members from their well-chronicled vacation on the Caribbean island of Anguilla to their usual summer base in Los Angeles.

Whether the timing of LeBron's landing was a signal that he will soon be a full-time fixture on the Hollywood scene or merely a dramatic travel tease before he chooses to stay in Northeast Ohio, James's latest workplace decision ensures seminal status for the free-agent summer of 2018.

An off-season headlined by King James is, by definition, unforgettable.

But disclaimers, I'm afraid, are required. The serial worrier in me can't resist issuing a stern caution to those who hunger for the modern-day Transaction Game as much as (or more than) the game itself.

Money will be tight in the free-agent marketplace, which opens Sunday at 12:01 a.m., Eastern Time. Really, really tight.

Therefore, the frenzy so many of us savored a year ago, when the starry likes of Chris Paul, Jimmy Butler, Paul George, Kyrie Irving and Carmelo Anthony scored new addresses, won't be easily replicated.

The prospect of James signing with the Los Angeles Lakers — as many front offices would forecast if they were forced into a binding prediction — and the Kawhi Leonard saga in San Antonio should be enough to satiate those captivated by the N.B.A.'s growing reputation as the most heated of hot stove leagues.

Just understand that those adventures may have to be enough to satisfy those desperate for drastic change.

It has been hard to ignore the whispers steadily rising in volume for the past month that George, the All-Star forward, is strongly considering signing a two- or three-year deal to stay with the Oklahoma City Thunder.

The Houston Rockets, meanwhile, are widely expected to simply focus on re-signing their free agents Paul and Clint Capela in hopes of bringing back essentially the same team that fell just one win short of an N.B.A. finals berth. They're scarcely even mentioned anymore as a potential James destination.

The current climate, in general, offers scant hope of fireworks. Only eight teams have the ability to create salary-cap space that exceeds the league's estimated $8.6 million midlevel exception — and at least three of those teams (Atlanta, Chicago and Sacramento) are likely to use their cap space to try to facilitate trades and acquire future draft picks instead of chasing free agents.

Of the eight, only the Lakers and the Philadelphia 76ers are regarded as contenders for players in the James-George-Leonard tier; Dallas, Phoenix and Indiana are the other cap-room teams. Many clubs are looking ahead to the 2019 off-season, when the salary cap is projected to rise to the $108 million range, from roughly $101 million, and half of the league should have cap space.

The Knicks' president, Steve Mills, in a radio interview with ESPN's Stephen A. Smith, announced that New York did not plan to give free agents anything other than one-year contracts to maintain maximum financial flexibility for the summer of 2019. The Knicks, though, will hardly be alone when it comes to pitching short-term deals.

Even the mighty Lakers, flush with spending money, aren't quite sure what they can accomplish in the month ahead.

Magic Johnson, at a news conference where he expounded on the Lakers' free-agent strategy, made a case that the only team in the league with the cap room to sign two stars outright would still need "two summers" before he could be fairly judged as the team's top executive.

Just two years removed from the wild (some would say reckless) spending in the summer of 2016 after the salary cap jumped a record $24 million because of an influx of television revenue, here's an indication of how hamstrung many teams feel by luxury-tax concerns and the like: There were no trades during this year's draft involving current N.B.A. players. That hasn't happened, according to research by ESPN's Kevin Pelton, since 2003.

But those are all post-LeBron concerns. Nothing else matters much until James has landed.

You'll recall that in his first two stints as a free agent — in 2010 and 2014 — James announced his destinations on July 8 and 11. League traffic tends to come to a standstill while he deliberates.

Perhaps his decision-making will be faster this time. Perhaps not. Either way, James's fate — as well as how the teams chasing him respond to whatever he does — will dominate discussion along with the potential resolution of San Antonio's season-long Kawhi crisis.

I will continue to say that James owes the Cavaliers nothing, and has nothing to fear about damaging his legacy, if he decides to leave Cleveland again, after delivering in 2016 the championship he promised. I also reject the notion that James will pick the Lakers only if Leonard or George, or both, will join him.

Remember: The most definitive thing we know so far about James's free-agency leanings is his disclosure after the finals that family considerations will play a bigger role than they have before. If his family decides Los Angeles is where it wants to be full time, it's not difficult to envision James making the leap with great belief that his presence will help Magic flank him with the requisite help eventually, if not immediately.

My biggest questions beyond LeBron:

Can the 76ers win the trade sweepstakes for Leonard, since it looks as though their dreams of James or George were just that?

Will the Boston Celtics cash in some of those shiny assets they've stockpiled to spring another Irving-size summer surprise?

Is the marketplace as grim as it looks for the All-Star big man DeMarcus Cousins after he tore his Achilles?

What happens to restricted free agents such as Aaron Gordon, Jabari Parker and Zach LaVine?

And what about the two-time defending champions from Golden State? The Warriors, for the record, continue to insist that they will not be pursuing Dwight Howard in free agency despite persistent rumblings to the contrary. So how will they revamp their bench after wrapping up their long-anticipated new deal with Kevin Durant?

I know what it's like for the Transaction Game groupies out there. You're going to be breathlessly following along no matter what. You're hooked.

Just be sure to brace yourself for the possibility that it will be a summer light on landscape-changing business.

LeBron James Joining Lakers on 4-Year $154 Million Deal

BY MARC STEIN AND SCOTT CACCIOLA | JULY 1, 2018

AFTER HELPING THE CITY of Cleveland banish a championship curse that spanned 52 years, LeBron James has found his next challenge: Rescuing the Los Angeles Lakers from the most unsuccessful period in the storied franchise's history.

In what has become an every-four-years ritual for the three-time N.B.A. champion, James has chosen to switch teams in free agency for the third time in his career. He announced Sunday night that he was leaving his home-state Cleveland Cavaliers for a second time and joining the fallen giants in Los Angeles.

The Lakers have long been considered the league's most glamorous team, but they have missed the playoffs each of the last five seasons — the longest such drought they have endured. It prompted the Lakers' controlling owner, Jeanie Buss, to hire one of the team's all-time greats, Magic Johnson, as president of basketball operations in February 2017 with the specific goal of luring the sport's biggest name to Hollywood at the top of their wish list.

James's destination, then, was not entirely surprising, but the timing and manner in which he made his next stop known were certainly unexpected. Through a short news release issued by his agents at Klutch Sports on the first night of N.B.A. free agency, James announced at 8:05 p.m. that he would sign a four-year, $154 million contract with the Lakers.

It was a stark contrast to his first departure from Cleveland. In a widely panned television program on July 8, 2010 — known as "The Decision" — James revealed his controversial move from Cleveland to the Miami Heat, which prompted scores of Cavaliers fans to turn on the native of nearby Akron, Ohio. In 2014, after winning two championships in Miami, James waited until the 11th day of free agency to disclose his plans to leave the Heat and return to the team that drafted him in a Sports Illustrated essay titled "I'm Coming Home." James has no immediate plans to hold a news conference to discuss this move; his next scheduled public appearance is July 30 in Akron.

A four-time N.B.A. most valuable player, James has led Eastern Conference teams to eight consecutive N.B.A. finals, with Cleveland's title in 2016 bringing the city its first major sports crown since football's Cleveland Browns in 1964 before the advent of the Super Bowl. Moving to the Lakers will send James, 33, to the Western Conference for the first time as he enters his 16th season.

He took to Instagram to say goodbye to Cavaliers fans, posting a picture of Cleveland's 2016 championship parade with the caption: "Thank you Northeast Ohio for an incredible 4 seasons. This will always be home."

Los Angeles, though, has also become a summer home to James; his wife, Savannah; and their three children. James made it clear after the Cavaliers suffered a four-game sweep against the Golden State Warriors in the N.B.A. finals last month that family considerations would factor into his free-agency thinking more than ever before, which appears to have greatly enhanced the Lakers' chances of luring him away from his Cleveland comfort zone.

The Lakers, even with James, will not be considered a top contender at the Warriors' level. They sport a roster filled mostly with younger cornerstones — including Kyle Kuzma, Brandon Ingram and the polarizing guard Lonzo Ball — and a young coach in Luke Walton who was selected in the same N.B.A. draft as James in 2003 and played 10 professional seasons.

But by agreeing to a four-year contract, James essentially acknowledged that the Lakers would need time to build a title-worthy team around him. After Johnson visited James at one of his Los Angeles residences Saturday night for three hours once the league's free agency period opened, James was willing to afford the franchise that time.

The Lakers' free-agency victory came after they had failed in their attempts to lure the All-Star Paul George away from the Oklahoma City Thunder. They have also been stymied in their efforts thus far to persuade the San Antonio Spurs to trade them the All-Star forward Kawhi Leonard. None of that, however, prevented James from moving quickly. James's new contract contains a player option for the 2021-22 season that ensures that he will be a Laker for at least three seasons before he can return to free agency.

Only one team had the ability to pay James a five-year maximum contract worth $207 million: the Cavaliers. His departure will now force the Cleveland owner Dan Gilbert, with whom James has maintained a chilly relationship, to decide whether to try to reload around his last remaining All-Star, Kevin Love, or to explore trading Love to launch a rebuilding program in earnest.

Despite his departure, James's recent tenure in Cleveland remains a comeback story for the ages — in a literal sense. After spending the first seven seasons of his professional career with the Cavaliers, James had left for Miami as a free agent in 2010 to team up with Chris Bosh and Dwyane Wade. It was a productive partnership for James — the Heat had a dominant four-year run — but he left the Cavaliers in ruins. Without him, they were one of the worst teams in the N.B.A.

But in a ballyhooed move, he returned to the Cavaliers in 2014, pledging to deliver a championship. He made good on his promise. James led the Cavaliers to four straight finals appearances — business as usual for him. He has become a postseason staple — and a boon for the league, which has seldom, if ever, produced a player who so effortlessly combines strength and finesse, a 6-foot-8 forward who has the body of a bulldozer and the mind of a professor.

James appeared to have a solid partnership in Cleveland with Kyrie Irving, the All-Star point guard who was drafted by the Cavaliers in 2011. But last summer, Irving shocked the league — and James — by requesting a trade, in part, it appeared, so that he could escape James's shadow. The Cavaliers honored Irving's request by sending him to the Boston Celtics, who instantly became a contender in the East, in exchange for Isaiah Thomas and others.

Without Irving, the Cavaliers struggled for long stretches last season, even as James assembled one of the finest seasons of his career. He averaged 27.5 points, 8.6 rebounds and 9.1 assists per game, shooting 54.2 percent from the field. He also played in all 82 regular-season games for the first time in his career.

But the Cavaliers experimented with different lineups, overhauling their roster more than once, and the point guard position was a grease fire at times. Thomas was hindered by a bad hip and was eventually traded to the Lakers. The Cavaliers traded for George Hill ahead of the playoffs, but he, too, was slowed by injuries. The result was a hodgepodge season that James said was one of the most challenging of his career.

That James still managed to drag the Cavaliers into the finals — again — was nothing short of heroic, even if it ended in a sweep by the Warriors in a series that felt anticlimactic.

His departure this time, too, was less dramatic, cushioned by the memory of the 2016 title. The city of Akron, via its Twitter feed, thanked James "from the bottom of our hearts" on Sunday for the financial and civic contributions he had made in that community since returning to the Cavaliers four years ago. After midnight, Gilbert issued a statement paying tribute to James, taking a much different tone than he did in the infamous letter that blasted a 25-year-old James for leaving in 2010.

"LeBron, you came home and delivered the ultimate goal," Gilbert wrote on Sunday, thanking him for "a championship that united generations of Clevelanders, both living and past."

Gilbert added: "Nothing but appreciation and gratitude for everything you put into every moment you spent in a Cavaliers uniform. We look forward to the retirement of the famous #23 Cavs jersey one day down the line."

The Philadelphia 76ers were also granted an opportunity Sunday morning to make a pitch to James's agent Rich Paul, but it appears the short list of potential destinations came down to the two cities where James has ties: Cleveland and Los Angeles. In the end, he decided to join that string of all-time greats — including Wilt Chamberlain, Kareem Abdul-Jabbar and Shaquille O'Neal — and make his way to the Lakers midcareer. The job in James' case, though, calls on him to restore some luster to the franchise.

LeBron James to the Lakers: There's Much to Unpack Here

BY MARC STEIN | JULY 2, 2018

PERHAPS YOU'VE SEEN the stunning statistic that's been making the N.B.A. rounds. If not: LeBron James is about to somehow become the sixth player among the top eight scorers in league history to play for the Los Angeles Lakers.

No. 1 Kareem Abdul-Jabbar. No. 2 Karl Malone. No. 3 Kobe Bryant. No. 5 Wilt Chamberlain. No. 8 Shaquille O'Neal.

And now, No. 7 James.

Maybe you're not even surprised. The next megastar is seemingly always looming for the Lakers. They will forever get the best players. Right?

Here's the secret that the Lakers don't like to share: They haven't been so sure lately. They were deeply and undeniably worried, perhaps for the first time in the team's L.A. existence. This is why the Lakers' controlling owner, Jeanie Buss, felt the need to abruptly fire her brother Jim and the club's long-serving general manager, Mitch Kupchak, in February 2017. With Jim Buss and Kupchak in charge of basketball operations, Jeanie had begun to lose faith that a day like Sunday was in the Lakers' future.

The playoff drought that ate away at Jeanie's more customary optimism had stretched to a franchise-record five seasons in a row by the time the N.B.A.'s free-agent summer of 2018 began. Only this time, with Magic Johnson installed as the Lakers' lead recruiter, James would be courted by a kindred spirit.

How many times over the years have you heard that sizing up James and Johnson, in terms of on-court traits, is a more apt comparison than measuring James against Michael Jordan? The first extended face-to-face conversation of their lives, shortly after the free agency period began, led to a partnership less than 24 hours later, pitching together two supersized playmakers — one former and one current — who likewise share big off-court dreams and no shortage of social awareness.

Yet one suspects that the Lakers, deep down, realize this was as much (if not more) about Tinseltown's magic dust than Magic's. Whether it's for family comfort, business aspirations or the scrumptious weather, James clearly likes the idea of being in Hollywood at this stage of his life. His new team, as currently constructed, is not going to trouble the Golden State Warriors. But there are too many pluses, on James's scorecard, to worry about that or the fact that the night before he joined the Lakers will be remembered for the All-Star forward Paul George spurning the Lakers to stay in Oklahoma City

We can't say it often enough: This is the Player Power Era in the N.B.A., and James is its foremost flexer. He has zero interest in listening to our rules, our conventional wisdom, our anything.

James naturally wants more rings and surely believes that the Lakers will keep making moves to build the sort of squad that can actually help him win his fourth — presumably by continuing their efforts to trade for Kawhi Leonard. But he's also not going to force himself to go to Philadelphia in the name of an easier playoff path if he and his family would rather live in Southern California. I've consistently said that I wouldn't dare leave the ever-forgiving Eastern Conference if I were him, but it should be pretty clear by now that he has little interest in external opinions. I'm not sure he even hears the debate-show shouters anymore.

LeBron will readily leave the legacy debates to everyone else and, if my instinct is right, enjoy how much chaos his choice has caused on a zillion basketball fronts. The Western Conference is now home to all seven active M.V.P.s in the league: James Harden, Russell Westbrook, Stephen Curry, Kevin Durant, Dirk Nowitzki and Derrick Rose. That list doesn't even include Anthony Davis, Jimmy Butler, Donovan Mitchell and two more Golden State All-Stars: Klay Thompson and Draymond Green. The gulf between the conferences, which seemingly dates to Jordan's second retirement with the Chicago Bulls in 1998, has never looked wider.

Things might be even more grim for Clevelanders and their Cavaliers, who have now lost the game's best player twice and have to live with the knowledge that the Cavs' ill-fated acquisitions of Jordan Clarkson and Larry Nance Jr. in February that were designed to try to save their season helped the Lakers create the salary-cap space needed to pilfer James from them.

Another uncomfortable truth: The Lakers might have already won the summer by dominating the James sweepstakes, but the Warriors can't really lose it if the other 29 teams out there haven't legitimately closed the gap by the time training camps open in late September.

The Lakers themselves, frankly, still have a few questions to answer, after following up the James coup by immediately coming to terms with the world's foremost LeBron irritant: Lance Stephenson. How James and Lonzo Ball's infamously vocal father LaVar coexist in the same ZIP code is another source of considerable curiosity, which explains why a number of rival teams already expect the Lakers to try to ship Lonzo Ball out at the first opportunity.

So, yes, there is much to unpack here.

But we have time to get into all that. The Summer of LeBron doesn't usually move this quickly. Let the magnitude of the moment sink in for at least a few more days before the fretting begins in earnest.

James didn't win a championship in his first season with Miami, nor did he win it all in his first season after going back to Cleveland for his second stint with the Cavaliers. If he's easing into another new arrangement, as signing a four-year deal with the Lakers would suggest, we don't have to have all the answers right away, either.

LeBron James Puts on a Lakers Uniform, and a Stoic Mask

BY KURT STREETER | SEPT. 24, 2018

EL SEGUNDO, CALIF. — It has been almost three months since LeBron James signed a free-agent deal to come to Los Angeles and join the Lakers.

Three months, more than enough time for N.B.A. fans and even the news media to prepare.

But it still seemed odd, even jolting, to see him at the team's training facility on Monday, speaking for the first time to a thick assemblage of reporters as a member of his new team, dressed in a purple-and-gold Lakers uniform affixed with No. 23.

This was media day, James's official unveiling. It was a chance for him to have a little fun if he wanted, a chance for him to publicly expand on his reasons for leaving Cleveland a second time and for joining a team he had long been attached to in rumors. Instead, before a media scrum probing for signs of deep excitement, hoping for new insight, James played the moment straight.

He sat at a black table for 15 minutes, holding a microphone in his left hand, casually leaning back in his chair.

He paid homage to the Lakers' history, the team's 16 N.B.A. titles and slew of all-time greats. (One of them, Magic Johnson, listened closely from a balcony nearby.) He talked of adhering to process — in fact, he talked of process a great deal.

Question: LeBron, as someone who has willed your teams to eight straight finals in the Eastern Conference, what are your expectations now that you have arrived in the West?

"My expectation is to try to get better every single day," he said, his voice measured. "What I know I can bring to the table is being committed to having excellence every single day, from a mind-set standpoint."

Question: Did you come here because of the chance to mix sports with the business side of Los Angeles?

Kyle Kuzma and Michael Beasley will play alongside James as he seeks his ninth consecutive appearance in the N.B.A. finals.

"My decision was based solely on my family and the Lakers," he said. "I am a basketball player. I play ball, that's what I do. That's what I live by, and when I do it at the level I do it at, everything takes care of itself."

Question: At this stage of your career, what brings about pressure?

"Nothing," James answered. "Nothing," he echoed, followed by a long pause.

There was more of this, but you get the picture.

James left the news conference and satisfied several appointed media engagements — talking to local radio for a while, recording a radio promotion, getting interviewed for ESPN.

Dozens of photographers and reporters shadowed his every scripted move. Meantime, the other Lakers sat for interviews. Veteran additions, like Rajon Rondo and Lance Stephenson. The young talent who played for Los Angeles last year: Lonzo Ball and Kyle Kuzma and Josh Hart.

LeBron James walks to his next interview at the U.C.L.A. Health Training Center during Media Day for the Los Angeles Lakers.

Few seemed to notice them. This was James's show, as it will be all season. But none of them seemed bothered. In fact, they seemed to relish the chance to play along his side. Or, in the case of Coach Luke Walton, to help guide a James-led team.

Walton said his new star's tight-lipped tone was intentional. Practice begins on Tuesday. The regular season begins next month.

"He knows what time it is," said Walton, a former Lakers player who was teammates with Kobe Bryant. "He's setting the tone that it is time to come to work. There is definitely that look that I've seen before."

A reporter asked which player he was alluding to.

"Ronny Turiaf," Walton cracked, referring to perhaps the Lakers' most effervescent and fun-loving player in 2008, when they lost to the Boston Celtics in the finals.

It was the day's one shining moment of levity.

LeBron James Has Plenty of Patience. For Now.

BY SCOTT CACCIOLA | OCT. 19, 2018

PORTLAND, ORE. — LeBron James spent much of his first game with the Los Angeles Lakers pointing. He pointed at teammates. He pointed at spots on the floor where he wanted his teammates to move. He pointed at opposing players whom he wanted his teammates to defend. He pointed at the ball so that his teammates would pass it to him.

After storming to the basket for a dunk, he even pointed to the crowd — with both fingers, smoking-pistols style. Just to mix things up.

As much as James dribbles and shoots and soars and scores, he is a constant communicator. His approach is not always gentle or nuanced. He points with authority.

But even by his own standards, built up over the course of 14-plus seasons, James is probably doing more communicating than usual right now, because the Lakers are new to him, and he is new to them. So he points during games, and he talks about patience between them.

"That's all I've been preaching since the season started," he said, "since we got back to work, that it was going to take patience from our team, from all of us, just to figure out one another, to figure out what we're good at, to figure out what we're not so good at and get better at it."

There is ample room for improvement from the LeBron-era Lakers, who were christened with a 128-119 loss to the Portland Trail Blazers on Thursday night. The Lakers will return to work on Saturday night in their home opener against the Houston Rockets, who merely won a franchise-record 65 games last season. Welcome to the Western Conference, LeBron.

James has appeared in eight consecutive N.B.A. finals, first with the Miami Heat, then with the Cleveland Cavaliers, but the dynamic is different for him this season. The Lakers are unlikely contenders, not yet anyway. Even making the playoffs is no sure thing.

The Lakers have lots of young talent (Kyle Kuzma, Brandon Ingram, Josh Hart, Lonzo Ball), along with a hodgepodge of veterans on one-year contracts, but their defense and outside shooting are suspect. Consider: They missed their first 15 3-pointers against Portland.

For his part, Coach Luke Walton acknowledged that the Lakers needed work, because of course they do, but he was noticeably upbeat at his news conference.

All those errant 3-pointers? "They were good shots," he said.

How about the team's style of play? "I liked our pace," he said.

What did he think of James's first game? "I'm glad he's on our team," he said.

In fairness, it is too early to make judgments about the season, but there is a reason James has been using the p word — patience — so much in recent weeks. He is guarding against expectations. He understands the challenges ahead. It is also not the worst strategy to inoculate the team's more inexperienced players against undue pressure.

After Thursday's loss, he was asked about chemistry — specifically, how long it would take for this group to coalesce. He was noncommital with his response.

"Not as fast as you guys think it's going to happen," he said. "I always kind of compare it to instant oatmeal. It's not that fast. It takes awhile for the chemistry to get to where you can close your eyes and know exactly where your guys are. So that's what we're going to work toward."

James cited several sequences from the game where that lack of chemistry — that absence of knowing where his guys were — was evident to him. There was one play, he said, when he expected Kuzma to pop off a screen, but Kuzma rolled to the basket instead and James threw the ball out of bounds. There was another play, he said, when Rajon Rondo was driving baseline and threw a pass to James that JaVale McGee thought was intended for him. Another miscommunication. Another turnover. There was a lot of that.

"We're literally less than a month in," James said, referring to the start of training camp in September. "So it's still early. We've got to go through some things, go through some adversity, see how guys react to it, and see what gets guys going. For me, it's an everyday thing. Leadership is not a sometimes thing. It's an everyday thing."

It is worth noting that each time James has gone to a new team — four times in all, starting with the Cavaliers straight out of high school — that team has endured growing pains. Even when he joined the supercharged Heat as a free agent in 2010, they lost eight of their first 17 games and had a five-game losing streak in March. They wound up reaching the finals. Later, when James returned to the Cavaliers in 2014, they lost seven of their first 12. They reached the finals, too.

After Game 1 with the Lakers, James was asked if he would be forgiving with the team's younger players: Would he give them a pass early on? It was a fair question. After all, of all the adjectives used to describe him over the years, patient — no matter how many times he wants to use the word — is not the first that comes to mind.

It is true, James said, that many of his teammates simply need more experience, and that experience comes only with time.

"But you don't get a pass for not practicing excellence every day," he said, "and trying to be great every day."

James will make those judgments, which is one of the reasons the Lakers are so intriguing. No one knows quite what to expect from them. No one, not even James.

LeBron James Returns to Cleveland, and Lakers Come Back to Win

BY MARC STEIN | NOV. 21, 2018

CLEVELAND — The rest of the Los Angeles Lakers were already on the floor, as were the Cleveland Cavaliers, when LeBron James finally burst out of a tunnel at 7:56 p.m. Wednesday night to join the pregame layup lines.

The expectant crowd at Quicken Loans Arena greeted the greatest player in Cavaliers history with a surge of warm applause.

Minutes later the noise level rose several notches when James was the last member of the Lakers' starting five to be introduced. A full-fledged, 30-second standing ovation for James followed when the Cavaliers played a "Thank You, LeBron" tribute video during the first timeout in the first quarter.

The atmosphere at The Q, as it's known, was tame for long stretches, but the locals even cheered several flashes of James's dominance as he amassed 32 points, 14 rebounds and 7 assists in the Lakers' eventual 109-105 comeback victory over the 2-14 Cavaliers.

The evening, in short, will stand in stark contrast to the pure and unrelenting vitriol heaped upon James nearly eight years ago, when he made his first appearance in this building as a member of the Miami Heat following his controversial free-agent move to South Beach in the summer of 2010.

"It just felt different from the time we landed yesterday," said James, who visited the "I Promise" school he helped found in his native Akron in the hours before the game.

"I'm a different person," James added. "We're all different from eight years ago.

"It's all about growth, and we all have grown from that moment eight years ago."

A theory began to gain steam during last season's N.B.A finals that fellow Northeast Ohioans were so appreciative of James's efforts, on and off the court, that they would ultimately bless the idea of their homegrown star leaving them in free agency for a second time. It's a theory which holds that James — after leading Cleveland to a championship in 2016 that ended the city's 52-year title drought — deserved some sympathy for the widening gap between the LeBron-led Cavaliers and the mighty Golden State Warriors.

This night was the first tangible evidence that the basketball romantics were right. This was a happy homecoming.

It didn't hurt that the Cavaliers, who fired Coach Tyronn Lue after an 0-6 start to the season and this week sent the veteran guard J.R. Smith away from the team, committed zero turnovers in the first half and managed to take a 96-87 lead into the final seven minutes of regulation. The Lakers ultimately recovered to hold off the team sporting the league's worst record, and in doing so improved to 10-7. But to win they needed 11 fourth-quarter points from James and had to survive a clean look at a tying 3-pointer in the final minute from Cleveland guard Kyle Korver after James made only 1 of 2 free throws.

Cedi Osman had 21 points and five 3-pointers to lead the Cavaliers in what will likely go down, all things considered, as one of the more satisfying nights of Cleveland's trying season.

Hints of a much more benign reception for James than he received on Dec. 2, 2010, were actually plentiful in the buildup to the occasion. The only mention of the N.B.A. on the front page of Wednesday's Cleveland Plain Dealer, for example, was a tease to a story that the Cavaliers have exiled Smith from the team until they can trade him.

The downtown streets were cold and quiet in the daytime hours leading up to tipoff, devoid of James-related signage. You had to strain to see any trace of LeBron-related hoopla until night fell.

The Cavaliers said that, as far as security precautions, pregame measures were "one step beyond" a typical regular-season game but well shy of the weekslong plan hatched in conjunction with the league and even federal authorities before the caldron James's return produced in 2010.

It was likewise impossible to miss that the giant LeBron banner across the street from the arena, which had draped one side of Sherwin-Williams' global headquarters since James returned to the Cavaliers from the Miami Heat before the 2014-15 season, has been replaced by a more generic banner bearing ALL FOR THE LAND messaging.

Yet it became clear, once the arena began to fill up with James jerseys galore, that the atmosphere would be welcoming. Rich Paul, James's agent, was so sure of it that he flew Wednesday to Philadelphia instead to monitor the showdown between two of his other high-profile clients: Anthony Davis of the New Orleans Pelicans and Ben Simmons of the Philadelphia 76ers.

The Cavaliers figure to take some solace in how hard they made the Lakers work to avoid an embarrassing defeat on James's big night, with consecutive 3-pointers from the former Lakers guard Jordan Clarkson enabling the hosts to stretch their lead to nine points at its peak in the final quarter.

Cleveland had four players in double figures — Osman, Clarkson (20 points), Tristan Thompson (14) and Collin Sexton (12) — but the narrow defeat surely only added to the bittersweet nature of James's return. Cleveland fans are well aware that the Cavaliers have not made the playoffs without James on the roster since 1998 — and they haven't won a playoff series without James since 1993.

"We have to recognize this is a big night for the city of Cleveland, because a hero has come back," Cavaliers Coach Larry Drew said roughly 90 minutes before the opening tip.

LeBron James Is the Change Fans Want to See in the Basketball World

BY SCOTT CACCIOLA | NOV. 22, 2018

James changed free agency forever the first time he left Cleveland. His second departure from the Cavaliers, for Los Angeles, shows how much he has changed, too.

CLEVELAND — The Los Angeles Lakers are not a great team, but they employ the greatest player in the world. They seem to be grasping the potential benefits of such an arrangement. LeBron James can compensate for many problems: lackluster defense, questionable decisions, growing pains.

"He comes out and plays the game pure," Coach Luke Walton said.

On Wednesday night, the difference between his presence (on the Lakers) and his absence (from the Cavaliers) was clear in his return to Cleveland, where fans came to Quicken Loans Arena to pay their respects to a bygone era — the LeBron Era. Without him, the Cavaliers are a bad team, one of the worst in the league. James feels for them.

"A lot of the guys have worked their tails off to get to where they are in their career," James said after the Lakers escaped with a 109-105 victory, "and you never want to see your friends be in the situation that they're in. But as professionals, they're still giving it all they got."

After decamping to Los Angeles in free agency over the summer, James belongs to the Lakers now — or perhaps they belong to him. They are not championship contenders, not yet anyway, but they are winning most of the games they should win and learning as they go.

"It's happening," Walton said, "and it's good to see it happening, but it's still the early stages of where we ultimately need to get to."

Their win against the Cavaliers was the latest example, a flawed effort that James mended by collecting 32 points, 14 rebounds and 7 assists. The Lakers, who improved to 10-7, have won six of their last seven games. Their progress was on display in front of James's old

LeBron James holds the reins of the Los Angeles Lakers now, but he has changed Cleveland — and its fans have changed him — in ways that will last for years to come.

fans and teammates and coaches, who are familiar with his ability to elevate those around him.

"He's done this everywhere he's gone," Cavaliers Coach Larry Drew said. "He's such a dominant force."

The game — billed as a homecoming — was free of the vitriol that was directed toward James in 2010, when he made his first trip back to Cleveland as a freshly minted member of the Miami Heat. Back then, James and his teammates actually feared for their safety. Skirmishes broke out in the stands. James scored 38 points in a lopsided win.

On Wednesday, the crowd was appreciative, offering him a warm welcome, albeit one tinged with sadness. No one booed. No one threw anything. People just missed him.

Jay Ventura, 23, and Natalie Miller, 20, college students from Akron, Ohio, James's hometown, bought tickets for the game over the summer, when they first became available. They wore James jerseys

"I appreciate these fans," James said, "just as much as they appreciate me."

that were half Lakers and half Cavaliers, homemade homages to their favorite player.

"It's a little bittersweet," Ventura said, "but it's different now. He did everything he said he was going to do for us, you know? He delivered his promise."

That promise was fulfilled in 2016: a championship, the Cavaliers' first and only. Clips of their title run were included in a video montage that the team played during the first timeout of Wednesday's game, not long after a reminder that fans were entitled to free chicken nuggets if the Cavaliers scored at least 100 points. (Not all was lost in the end.)

In any case, James was touched by the gesture. He saw only part of the montage — Walton, he said, was drawing up a play in the huddle, and James did not want to mess it up — but he raised his arms to acknowledge the crowd after the timeout and clasped his hands together in a sign of gratitude.

This time, James returned to an arena of fans ready to celebrate him.

"I appreciate these fans," he said, "just as much as they appreciate me."

His departure from Cleveland has somehow enhanced his greatness, if that is possible. The Cavaliers, just months removed from a fourth straight trip to the N.B.A. finals, are 2-14. To be fair, Kevin Love has missed all but four games because of a foot surgery — but still, it is a dismal scene here. Before Wednesday's game, Drew had to address J.R. Smith's recent accusation that the Cavaliers had been actively trying to lose to improve their chances of landing a top pick in next year's draft — tanking, in other words. Smith is no longer with the team.

"My guys are playing hard," Drew said, "and when they're not playing hard, I make them aware that they're not playing hard."

The Lakers, though, are improving by the week. Forgotten is their early-season brawl with the Houston Rockets. Fading are James's woes from the free-throw line, though they remain a bit of an issue.

James has alternately struggled and thrived at the free-throw line this season with the Lakers, and throughout his career.

It seems almost quaint to recall that team president Magic Johnson chastised Walton when the Lakers stumbled to a 3-5 start.

Little about their season has been particularly easy, and after surviving suspensions stemming from the aforementioned brawl, the Lakers are adjusting to life without point guard Rajon Rondo, who broke his hand last week. Adding the veteran center Tyson Chandler has helped, because he is a respected voice in the locker room and a fierce defender.

But the Lakers are inexperienced, and Chandler cited the importance of young players like Kyle Kuzma and Lonzo Ball as the team moves forward.

"All of these games are good because we're so young," Chandler said. "The core of our team and what's going to be the deciding factor is our youth, our young players: Kuz, Lonzo, Brandon Ingram, Josh Hart. They're going to decide down the stretch what our season is going to really be like. It's going to be the development of them."

Cleveland fans are holding on to their James gear this time.

It helps, of course, that the Lakers have the ultimate mentor in James, whose brand of tough love can travel a fine line between abrasive and effective. But he has vowed to exercise patience this season, and Walton has been careful to highlight the players who are toiling in James's shadow.

After Wednesday's game, for example, Walton praised the play of Ball, the team's starting point guard, who finished with 15 points, 7 rebounds and 6 assists.

"I loved it," Walton said. "It was one of my favorite parts of our game — how much he was attacking the rim, even the ones he didn't finish. I didn't care. Just seeing him get downhill and be physical and play-make, he's so gifted with that. To see him kind of take that next step was really a positive for us."

In the locker room, James joined his teammates for a postgame meal that included hamburgers from Swensons, a chain that originated in Akron.

Dark days seem to be ahead for Cavaliers fans without James, but for one night they were able to cheer with him on the floor.

"We grew up on these things," said Randy Mims, James's childhood friend and longtime confidant.

James dressed in a T-shirt that read, "All Good Never Better," before leaving the arena for the airport and a long flight home.

MARC STEIN contributed reporting.

CHAPTER 3

Criticism and Challenges

LeBron James, for all his avoidance of controversy, has faced his fair share of criticism and challenges. With public attention comes inevitable scrutiny; both fans and pundits have compared James to his predecessors and sometimes find him lacking. James had to adjust to sharing the spotlight with other All-Star teammates before earning his own accolades in the N.B.A.

LeBron James's S.U.V. Prompts an Investigation

BY FRANK LITSKY | JAN. 14, 2003

LEBRON JAMES, A 6-foot-8 high school senior who is expected to be the No. 1 choice in the N.B.A. draft in June, is driving a new $50,000 sport utility vehicle. The Ohio High School Athletic Association says it wants to be sure the vehicle was a legitimate gift from his mother and not from an outsider.

An Ohio athletic association bylaw says an athlete loses amateur status by "capitalizing on athletic fame by receiving money or gifts of monetary value."

The vehicle is a pewter-colored Hummer H2 made by General Motors. James's version has three TV's and a hookup for computer games. The Cleveland Plain Dealer reported that James, who turned 18 on Dec. 20, received the vehicle as a birthday present from his mother, Gloria. His mother was said to have financed the purchase with a car loan.

James and his mother live in public housing in Akron, Ohio. Asked how she could secure such a loan, a person with knowledge of the family's situation who spoke on condition of anonymity said, "LeBron James is collateral enough."

That alluded to James's expected status as an N.B.A. millionaire within months. He has shown no interest in attending college. Sonny Vaccaro, an Adidas basketball representative, has said that James would probably earn $5 million a year from a sneaker contract alone.

The person said that the car was registered in Gloria James's name and that the family planned to provide documents of the loan to the Ohio High School Athletic Association.

"Maybe in New York or L.A. it wouldn't be such a huge deal," the person said. "But when a high schooler is driving a Hummer in Akron, it's a big deal."

James plays for St. Vincent-St. Mary High School, a 600-student Catholic school ranked first in the nation. After a victory Sunday, in which James scored 30 points, his mother would not discuss the vehicle purchase. "I've got nothing to say about that," she said.

Clair Muscaro, the commissioner of the Ohio High School Athletic Association, said the athletic association was concerned about the source of James's vehicle. According to The Associated Press, Muscaro said:

"If he has violated any of the rules, he would have to give up his amateur eligibility from the time the car was delivered. We have not yet talked to the school. We'll see if they know anything about it. I think it is important for our member schools to know what's going on."

Grant Innocenzi, the school's athletic director, apparently feels the same. He said the school, if asked by the association, would provide papers on the vehicle purchase.

"Our school officials will fully cooperate and expect our coaches, as well as the family, to act similarly," Innocenzi said.

Seldom has a high school basketball player received attention like James. Some of his games have been moved to college arenas. Some have been televised nationally on ESPN2. They are also available on pay-per-view for as much as $15 a game.

Dru Joyce II, James's high school coach, would not talk about the situation.

"We're just talking basketball," he said. "I'm a basketball coach and he's a basketball player."

Two Rookie Sensations Don't Make All-Star Cut

BY LEE JENKINS | FEB. 4, 2004

LEBRON JAMES AND Carmelo Anthony will finally have to wait for something.

James and Anthony played a combined one year of college basketball, were selected Nos. 1 and 3 in the N.B.A. draft and occupied much of the league's attention through the first half of the season. But when the reserves for the All-Star Game were announced yesterday, James and Anthony found themselves in an unfamiliar position. They were the kids who weren't picked.

"I was like, 'Oh, man, I should have been on there,' " Anthony said. "But it's my first year and I still have a long way ahead of me." He added: "Even though it's just the All-Star Game, it's much deeper than that. We'll take it as motivation. I probably deserved to make it, but things happen for a reason."

The N.B.A. generally rewards youth and potential over other things, but experience seems to count most in the All-Star selection process. The Nets' Kenyon Martin, who was angered when he was not selected last season, persisted this season and is headed to his first All-Star Game, on Feb. 15 at Staples Center in Los Angeles. So are Indiana's Ron Artest, Milwaukee's Michael Redd, New Orleans's Jamaal Magloire, Minnesota's Sam Cassell and Utah's Andrei Kirilenko. Those players, as different from one another as they may be, share one essential quality: they are not rookies.

"This is a great thing," Martin said yesterday. "It's exciting; something we were waiting for finally happened. It's good to have on your résumé."

The fans pick the starters, and they went with the veterans Allen Iverson (Philadelphia) and Tracy McGrady (Orlando) as the Eastern Conference guards, over James, who is averaging 20.8 points for

Cleveland. They also chose Tim Duncan (San Antonio) and Kevin Garnett (Minnesota) as the Western Conference starting forwards, over Anthony, who is averaging 19 points for Denver.

The two rookies had expected to fill out the roster, but the league's coaches vote for the reserves and they apparently decided that James and Anthony needed more time. After all, even Kobe Bryant was not an All-Star as a rookie. Yao Ming was last season, but he was voted in as a starter. Michael Jordan also went to the All-Star Game as a rookie, and this may be the ultimate sign of how far James has to go to validate comparisons to Jordan.

Before the announcement was made, James told The Associated Press: "Being on the All-Star team, it wouldn't be anything new to me. I've been on All-Star teams my whole life. I'd be very excited about it, but if it doesn't happen, it's not the end of the world."

He and Anthony will participate in the Rookie Challenge on the Friday of All-Star Weekend, then watch their elders play on Sunday. Jason Kidd (Nets) is back for his 7th All-Star appearance, Shaquille O'Neal (Lakers) for his 11th and Vince Carter (Toronto) for his 5th. The coaches also selected hard workers over high fliers, picking Sacramento's Brad Miller, Seattle's Ray Allen and Dallas's Dirk Nowitzki as reserves.

For the first time in 10 years, the Nets have more than one representative. Indiana also has two (Artest and the starter Jermaine O'Neal, as does Sacramento (Miller and Peja Stojakovic). Of course, the Lakers are sending their usual couple, Bryant and O'Neal, who should get the loudest cheers at Staples Center.

For the third time since 2001, the Knicks do not have a representative. New Orleans point guard Baron Davis is nursing a sprained left ankle, and if a replacement is needed, Stephon Marbury is a candidate. Marbury, who was traded to the Knicks from Phoenix last month, would have had a hard time in the Western Conference beating out Houston's Steve Francis, the starting point guard.

Because the West is so strong, Anthony said he had doubts about making the team, but he could not have imagined that James, his close friend, would also be shut out.

"It's disappointing that we're not going to have anyone there," Cavaliers General Manager Jim Paxson told The A.P. "For the players who are going, all of them with the exception of Paul Pierce are on teams with winning records."

James and Anthony have had their run of the league since they entered it. They are among the most marketable players in the N.B.A. The television ratings for the All-Star Game may suffer without them.

But they have to get in line behind some of their more experienced but lower-profile peers.

"You have to understand that there are steps to take," said Nets forward Richard Jefferson, a third-year player who warranted All-Star consideration. "Luckily, I learned from Kenyon's situation. You start to get some recognition, you're right there on the cusp. You've got to have a year when you're pretty close before you make that jump."

Young Guns Try Something New: Benchwarming

BY WILLIAM C. RHODEN | AUG. 25, 2004

HOW DO YOU AVOID becoming a team deferred?

As the United States men's basketball team continues its odyssey through Olympic competition, one of the intriguing subplots has been the difficult time that several of the team's young players have had in adjusting to bench duty. After leading their National Basketball Association teams in the regular season, Carmelo Anthony, Amare Stoudemire and LeBron James have been relegated to watching more than playing. After the United States routed Angola on Monday, James said that he could not think of the last time he did not start a game other than for injury-related reasons.

Fourth grade?

"Never," James said.

Third grade?

Surely there must have been a time in his athletic career that James did not start and did not play much, when he spent excruciating moments of embarrassment being a cheerleader on the bench.

"I've always started," James said. "Always, from Day 1.'"

Baseball?

"Everything, I always started," he said. "I ain't never come off the bench. I've never experienced it.

"It's an adjustment I have to make, Carmelo has to make, because stuff like that is going to happen on a mature team.

"I don't like that cliché, you lead by following. I've always been a leader, I've never been a follower, so I've kind of just done my job and did the best every time I go out and just try to be a leader." David Stern, the N.B.A. commissioner, spoke with James on Tuesday while the team enjoyed a day off as it prepared for its quarterfinal game against Spain on Thursday.

"He's all right," Stern said. "I think that when you're dealing with an all-star team of players of transcendent talent, they're going to have to get used to adapting to their roles: that's what teamwork is all about. And from that perspective, I think it's a great learning experience.

"This is a wonderful insight for them to travel internationally, to see how the other teams operate and to see what's necessary to win as a team. If the '92 Dream Team with a certain roster of Hall of Famers could make those adjustments, anyone should be able to make those adjustments."

Larry Brown, the United States coach, said: "When they picked the team, I told them it'd be great if we had some young kids on it. That's the future of our team; they can learn and appreciate. But they've had a hard time understanding."

Brown said he had talked with Stoudemire about accepting his role and told him not to feel down. "But I don't have to answer to a hundred people when he doesn't play," Brown said.

"But the other two guys," he added, referring to Anthony and James, "there's a hundred reporters saying: 'Well, why didn't you play?' How do you feel?' "

Brown had a heart-to-heart talk with Anthony about his situation.

"Carmelo told me, 'Coach, I've never been through this before; I've never come in the game at the end of the game,' " Brown said. "I said, 'Well, maybe you'll appreciate the guy that subs for you.' "

Has James learned anything from sitting on the bench? His body language in many of the games suggests that his leadership skills are sharper when he is on the floor. James dutifully tried to disagree.

"I'm just going to lead," he said, "no matter if I'm coming off the bench playing two minutes or coming off into the starting lineup 30 minutes. When I get on the court, I'm a leader."

James said he had grown in his year of professional basketball. "I'm better, my basketball game got better, my I.Q. got better," he said. "I'm a year into the game now. I'm a lot smarter now."

But a bench warmer, he is not.

Cavaliers Sinking,
Despite James's Efforts

BY HOWARD BECK | APRIL 15, 2005

CLEVELAND, APRIL 14 — The hip-hop blaring from the stereo in the home locker room was too loud for LeBron James to be heard. The matter was taken care of with a quick order to a Cleveland Cavaliers staff member.

"Turn that down," James, the Cavaliers' superstar, said.

The dial was spun too far to the left, however, and James had to clarify his demands.

"I didn't say turn it off," James chirped, and the music returned, at a more modest decibel level.

Twenty-year-old basketball legends generally get what they want, and what James does not get, he literally works overtime to obtain.

As he tries to save his team from a total collapse, James has played nearly every minute lately, but his efforts Thursday could not save Cleveland from a devastating 95-89 loss to the Knicks at Gund Arena.

The Cavaliers (40-38), who before their slide were fourth in the Eastern Conference, fell into a tie with Philadelphia for the seventh and eighth playoff spots. They are in danger of being caught by the Nets (38-40) and being knocked out of the postseason.

"We weren't playing like we were trying to have a playoff spot," James said.

It was a difficult night for James, who missed 18 of 25 field-goal attempts. But he finished with an impressive line: 27 points, 18 rebounds and 7 assists in 42 minutes.

If the Cavaliers fail, it will not be for lack of effort by James.

Before Thursday, he had averaged 45.5 minutes over 10 games. He had played all but one minute of the three previous games, and on

Thursday he broke the franchise record for minutes in a season. He has logged 3,200 minutes, passing Wes Person, who played 3,198 in the 1997-98 season.

Coach Brendan Malone insisted there are no worries about burning out James — "No, he gets stronger as the game goes on" — but not everyone is so sure.

"That's a big burden for him to come out and play 48 minutes and pretty much carry us into the playoffs," Cleveland's Lucious Harris said. "But the guy pretty much did it all year. He hates coming out of the game, I know that much."

For a player only two years removed from high school, one who already leads his team in points, assists and endorsements, it is another demand that needs to be met.

There is a lot riding on James's every move. The franchise has not seen the playoffs in seven years. And the demise of the Los Angeles Lakers has left the N.B.A. without one of its signature teams and signature stars, Kobe Bryant, to carry the postseason ratings.

Earlier this week, James filmed a promotional spot for the playoffs, on the hope or the belief that the ad will be relevant next week.

So James plays and plays. He has logged eight complete games this season, five in the last 11 games, including two 53-minute overtime efforts — the most complete games since Seattle's Gary Payton played 13 in the 1999-2000 season.

"I told my teammates, if they feel like I'm hurting them by playing all these minutes out there, then let me know," James said. "But me being on the court is always making an impact, and I'm not hurting them."

True enough, James is seeking to become the fifth player in league history — and the first since Michael Jordan in 1988-89 — to average more than 25 points, 7 rebounds and 7 assists.

But the young man known as King James is mortal after all and gently admitted: "I get tired. But I don't show it."

He looked it late Thursday, committing a careless turnover in the final minute that helped seal the loss. He went 2 of 10 from the field in the fourth quarter.

"The off-season is in a couple more months," James said, assuming a few playoff victories in his assessment. "So that's when I'll be able to relax."

That intensely narrow focus has been a hallmark of James's N.B.A. persona the past two seasons. He has needed every ounce of that focus lately. The Cavaliers changed owners in midseason (from Gordon Gund to Dan Gilbert) and, in response to the second-half decline, changed coaches last month (from Paul Silas to Malone).

The volatility has fueled rumors that James could seek a trade, or leave as a free agent. Spike Lee, the film director and Knicks season-ticket holder, recently suggested that James could become a Knick when he reaches unrestricted free agency in 2008.

Gilbert, the Cavaliers' garrulous new owner, did not hide his annoyance with the swirling speculation and with articles that suggested James could leave in two years.

"We hope he's here his whole career, and we'll do everything to make that happen," Gilbert said. "I am really surprised at some of the rumor mills in the sports world. I came from the financial world, where people didn't print false things."

A Statement Hits Home as Cleveland Stews

BY FRANK W. LEWIS | JULY 9, 2010

CLEVELAND — David Loomis, a marketing consultant and professor, is soft-spoken and friendly. His pleasant personal demeanor reflects his professional commitment to what might be described as holistic branding. He preaches that "marketing is everything we do," and among the guiding principles listed on his Web site are: "Build bridges," "Be diplomatic" and "Don't draw conclusions too early."

Now he might have to consider adding, "When all that fails, go ahead and tell them what you really think."

Even Loomis cheered the scathing response by the Cleveland Cavaliers owner Daniel Gilbert to LeBron James's announcement Thursday night that he was leaving Cleveland, after seven years, for the Miami Heat. Gilbert, who made his fortune with Rock Financial and Quicken Loans, issued a statement calling James's handling of his free agency "narcissistic," and his departure "cowardly."

The grammatical slips — "your hometown Cavaliers have not betrayed you nor NEVER will betray you" — and use of all capitals suggested that he had not shown it to anyone before posting it online.

"It's really unprecedented," said Loomis, who teaches brand strategy and consumer behavior at Case Western Reserve University. But it was on the money, he added, because the statement, however angry, cannot be separated from the context. Loomis compared James's intentionally high-profile announcement to "dumping your wife on a JumboTron."

James, Loomis said, "created that reaction in Gilbert, and I'm glad for it."

"Here's Cleveland, this struggling community, deprived of winning for so long, and our hero walks out on us," he said. "Then you have Gilbert's statement, which is really galvanizing."

He called Gilbert's anger an "appropriate response."

Loomis is not alone. From sports talk radio to social media to office chatter, many Clevelanders expressed both shock and glee over Gilbert's tirade.

Tony Rizzo, host of "The Really Big Show" on WKNR 850AM, an ESPN station, opened Friday morning by warning the national news media not to call him for comment on the mood of the region. "I'm only talking to Clevelanders today!" he announced, and the implication was clear: only Clevelanders could understand. Later he offered Gilbert, a native of Ohio rival Michigan, the highest possible praise. "He's one of us," he said.

Jon Silver, a regional sales manager for a plastics company and lifelong Cleveland sports fan, said Gilbert "said what all of us would have liked to say." He acknowledged that the comments could have consequences later, when the team tries to lure free agents, but added that it was "absolutely refreshing" to hear after James "went on national TV to slap us."

Dennis Roche, president of Positively Cleveland, the Northeast Ohio convention and visitors' bureau, said, "I thought both the timing and terseness of the message were right on point." He added that Gilbert "really put his thumb on it when he put it as coarsely as he did."

He likened Gilbert's defense of his adopted city to the "out-of-towner's perspective" that he sees all the time: visitors fall in love with Cleveland and cannot understand why residents seem so down on it.

"Why is Cleveland so often the butt of jokes?" Roche asked. "Because we let it be."

Some found Gilbert's behavior to be as regrettable as James's, but they understood the impulse.

"If I were the boss, and I got a resignation via television, I'd be pretty angry," said Subodh Chandra, a lawyer and former Cleveland law director. He called Gilbert's reaction understandable "but a bit graceless and over the top."

Gilbert doubled down in an interview with The Associated Press on Thursday night, accusing James of quitting in the playoffs and saying that people had covered up for him for too long. He did not elaborate, but every indication is that the team will finally pull back the curtain on its dealings with James and his inner circle. Rizzo stopped just short of promising jaw-dropping revelations when Gilbert appears on his show next week.

Gilbert chose not to face the local news media Friday afternoon, as interest in his comments rose to the level of James's announcement itself. But judging from the comments Friday afternoon of the team's new general manager, Chris Grant, and Coach Byron Scott, backpedaling is not an option.

"He is one of the most passionate owners in sports, and I think he's earned the right to voice his opinion," Grant said at a news conference.

Scott said, "I want an owner like that."

Still, on Friday night, the Cavaliers agreed to turn James's departure to Miami into a sign-and-trade deal that will allow James to make more money in his new contract and allow Cleveland to get some compensation — future draft picks from the Heat. Amid all the anger, some practicality intruded as the Cavaliers look to rebuild. But it was the anger, of course, that lingered, and the words of Daniel Gilbert that continued to echo.

LeBron James Is So Luminous, Yet So Trapped by the Public's Glare

BY HARVEY ARATON | JAN. 21, 2016

WITH EACH LOCATIONAL MOVE, celebrated or decried, the baggage has become a heavier burden. Glass has covered more and more of LeBron James's basketball house.

"That comes with the tag of being the best player," said James Jones, a member of King James's court in Cleveland and Miami. "It's fair to say that people take the temperature of his team, his entire situation, multiple times a day."

To illustrate his point, Jones gestured to the news media mob scene a few feet away in the visitors' locker room Wednesday night at Barclays Center. For the second time within hours, James was having to explain Monday's 34-point thrashing of the Cavaliers — on their home court — by the Golden State Warriors.

Streaks of rain on those big-picture windows, he called it; not necessarily foundational cracks.

"I think he gets frustrated with the repetitive nature of the questions," Jones said. "The people asking are very savvy — the reporters have been around this game a long time, and they know a lot. And so they ask the questions they already know the answer to.

"He says the same thing again and again — it's the same process we had in Miami, the same process the Spurs undertook, the same process the Warriors undertook. You look at every team; their situation requires patience and a process. We understand, and it's nothing personal, not unique to us."

But what is exclusive to James is the consistency and intensity of the scrutiny. With James, the questions too often sound like accusations. No other historically impactful N.B.A. luminary has been poked and prodded and proclaimed one extreme thing or another.

Not Michael Jordan. Not Kobe Bryant. Not Magic Johnson. Not

Larry Bird. Certainly not James's contemporaries, Carmelo Anthony, Chris Paul and Kevin Durant.

We do acknowledge that James came with a spotlight on his head — his high school games worthy of national television coverage — and a target on his back, tattooed with a self-indulgent decree, "Chosen 1." We understand he lives, unlike Jordan, in the age of Twitter, of endless mind reading, name-calling and noise making.

Many say James is no longer the best player. But that has only heightened the analysis and the anticipation that he will ultimately fail to meet expectations or fulfill his legacy — whatever that is and by whomever it has been imposed.

Of course, the critics know that this is, foremost, a team sport. But the world has to know: Has Stephen Curry taken something more intangible than the Most Valuable Player Award? Was Monday's rout more than a singular beat-down in a still-developing season?

Or was it more the symbolic rendering of James as Ronda Rousey, bloodied and perhaps permanently bowed?

At 31, in his 13th season, his hairline in steady retreat, James sounded a bit weary of being the daily tossup in the generic talk show after his Cavaliers took out their frustrations on the hapless and hopeless Nets, 91-78.

"I actually wish that teams would forget about us and the league would forget about us and, for the first time in my career, I could fly under the radar," he said.

There is no chance of that anytime soon, and James should know that the suffocating surveillance is partly a predicament of his own production. Had he never left the Cavaliers for the Heat, he would by now have won — or not — that ever-elusive championship for his beloved Northeast Ohio, and the story line would have become tired and worn. The herd would have moved on.

Going to Miami upped the self-promotional ante and made James the antihero, until he and the Heat delivered consecutive titles in the midst of four successive trips to the league finals. The return to

Cleveland has reinstated the must-win mandate — if only once, for the long-suffering masses. That weight may turn out to be even greater than the championship ring chase against Jordan and Bryant — by which the mythmakers would still have been evaluating James had he remained in Miami.

It is always going to be something with James, a lightning rod in a tell-all time, who has twice now rewritten the narrative, unlike Jordan, Bryant, Johnson and Bird. Excluding Jordan's two-year end-game fling in Washington, they all stayed in one city, one environment, respected and beloved for whatever they ultimately achieved.

In Chicago, Jordan set the modern, post-Bill Russell standard, with six titles. In Los Angeles, Johnson and Bryant each notched five. With a Hall of Fame cast, Bird managed three, but New England would fight you for merely suggesting he does not belong on his generation's Mount Rushmore.

Once upon a kinder, gentler time, Jerry West spent an entire career with the Lakers, salvaged one title from nine N.B.A. finals and took his place in the pantheon of wonderfulness as the inimitable Mr. Clutch.

Yes, Shaquille O'Neal led a late-career Gypsy's life, but he was cast more as comic book character than celluloid champion, and no dominant center — not even Kareem Abdul-Jabbar or especially the twice-traded Wilt Chamberlain — could ever match Russell's extraordinary record of 11 titles in 13 seasons.

In these ultimately unresolvable discussions, the quality of the teams — and their staunchest opposition — is always in play. Like it or not, James's teammates are under the daily microscope, too.

In Miami, Dwyane Wade's health and Chris Bosh's heart were constantly questioned. In Cleveland, it is Kyrie Irving's maturity and Kevin Love's mettle.

Maybe they are good enough; maybe they are not. At a morning practice Wednesday, James complained that people wanted teams to "come together like instant oatmeal." He continued: "Throw it in the microwave — in 30 seconds, it's done, ready to go. It doesn't work that way. You need time, and you need adversity together. You need hardships. You need times when you don't like each other. You need the worst of times in order to become really good."

No argument there, even if it's already been forgotten that James's Heat had a variety of in-season struggles, and last season's Cavs got off to a 19-20 start before losing in the N.B.A. finals to the Warriors after leading, two games to one.

Conveniently ignored in the latest sounding of alarms: On Thursday night, Irving played in only his 15th game — a 115-102 victory over the Los Angeles Clippers — since recovering from knee surgery; the trade deadline looms next month with the possibility of roster upgrades; and, oh, right, the Warriors and the matchup nightmares they pose for Love are probably less certain of getting out of the West than the Cavs are of surviving the East.

"We're going to keep playing, keep building, and if we get there, you'll know," Jones said, referring to the pursuit of the higher — or highest — level.

If they don't, we'll know and hear about that, too. As Jones said, multiple times a day.

One Thing LeBron James Can't Win: A Comparison With Michael Jordan

BY HARVEY ARATON | MAY 28, 2017

BEFORE SUPPLANTING Michael Jordan as the N.B.A.'s career playoff scoring leader while cementing an extraordinary seventh straight trip to the league finals, LeBron James pleaded for comparative restraint, for a focus on the here (Stephen Curry and Kevin Durant) and now (Game 1, Thursday night).

It's all about the ring, about Cleveland and Golden State.

The Jordan-versus-James debate, he said, is only "great for barbershops." Bar stools, too, and press boxes.

But with a keen sense of the real world, James understands that the Jordan argument is not for him to make, because it's one he can't win, even should he engineer a second straight upset of the Warriors.

Jordan, a six-time champion, is a historic figure whose imperfections have been blurred or whitewashed by time. James, a three-time titlist, operates in a more polarized environment that breeds stubborn and even illogical resentments he is loath to counter by mimicking Jordan's down-the-middle marketing brand.

Make the strongest case for James to be conferred a more widespread Jordanian acclaim, and it will inevitably fall upon a healthy percentage of deaf ears.

"No drugs, no gambling, no known domestic issues, but there's still something that prevents him becoming that all-around hero," said Charles Grantham, who guided the National Basketball Players Association for much of the Jordan era, and is currently the director of a sports-management program at Seton Hall.

He added, "But the times are different, too, and you have to give credence to that."

To begin with, James is confronting millions of fans unlikely to abandon the belief that what they witnessed in their most rabid rooting years is unmatchable.

Go argue with the Wall Street banker who watched Jordan drop 55 on the Knicks at Madison Square Garden in the fifth game of a March 1995 comeback after nearly two basketball-free years. Try to convince the "Space Jam" generation that Jordan really couldn't stretch his limbs beyond the limits of human capability.

"Almost a god" is the way James described his own adoration of Jordan when he was an 11-year-old in 1996 — the year when "Space Jam," the part-animation film starring Jordan and the Looney Tunes cast, opened.

There is also a significant difference in the way Jordan and James have been physically perceived. Jordan, at 6 feet 6 inches, took the baton from Magic Johnson and Larry Bird and blew away the long-standing conviction that basketball was, and always would be, dominated by the tallest of the tall.

At 6-8, with about a 30-pound edge on the midcareer Michael, James entered the league as a muscular 19-year-old who quickly redefined the corporal attributes of the multidimensional star.

He emerged as a hybrid of Magic and Michael, with some Karl Malone, too. And as Grantham said, "He has leveraged his talent and power, on court and off."

That James dictated the terms of his preps-to-pros arrival separated him immediately from Jordan, who played by the established rules. He remained in college for three years. Excluding a comeback with Washington three years after leaving the Bulls, he never challenged the league's preference for its stars to stay with their original teams, and he did not venture into front-office moves. He mostly refused to take stands against political or social malfeasance.

Those were his choices, his values, his right. Again, in a different cultural setting, abetted by social media, James has created his own operational paradigm. He has weaponized free agency, or the mere threat of it, orchestrated his departures, staged his decisions.

He has thrust himself into the realm of labor management and managed to bathe in corporate coffers while shedding the contractual restraints that were wholly accepted by Jordan.

"LeBron James has drawn up the blueprint for not being muzzled, bridled or led around," said Len Elmore, who, after his playing career, has been a player agent, the director of the National Basketball Retired Players Association and a television analyst.

"We're in a different era now than when Michael played, and LeBron has had smarter advisers, more tools. That's frightening or alienating for people who find it distasteful for a young guy — and one without a college education — to be wielding that kind of power, especially on the political side."

Yes, James has spoken out on polarizing sociopolitical issues and even attached himself to Hillary Clinton near the end of her presidential campaign. But many other N.B.A. personalities have participated in raising the league's profile in that regard.

And while Grantham said, "There's always a racial component to factor into these things," he, like Elmore, agreed that the resistance to James was more rooted in other factors.

"In sports, you go back to the whole amateur-versus-professional issue, the denial of these young players' earning potential in order to keep product and price under control," Grantham said. "The colleges cash in, the value of the pro franchises skyrocket, but if the players try to fight for what they are worth, many fans can't believe what they are complaining about."

In effect, he was saying that more than Curry, more than Durant and certainly more than Jordan, the hero that is James may always have an antihero partner running parallel because that's his burden, and his cause.

LeBron James Is a One-Man Show. Sometimes That Is the Problem.

BY SCOTT CACCIOLA | APRIL 24, 2018

CLEVELAND — Kyle Korver was explaining one of the Cleveland Cavaliers' core philosophies this season: The job of everyone on the team not named LeBron James is to put LeBron James in position to do the things LeBron James does as the best basketball player on the planet.

"We all know the narrative around us: It's 'Bron, and we're all trying to make it work for him," Korver, a shooting guard, said on Tuesday. "But I don't want to make too much of it, because we don't need to overthink it. We need to go out there and play basketball."

If only it were that simple in the playoffs.

It has always seemed to be about more than just basketball with these Cavaliers, who have overhauled their roster (more than once), dealt with the temporary absence of their head coach and coped with the prying eyes of TMZ. They have done all these things while trying to navigate their way to a fourth straight appearance in the N.B.A. finals, even as James's future hangs like smog over the franchise.

For now, the Cavaliers would settle for a victory against the Indiana Pacers on Wednesday night in Game 5 of their first-round series, which is tied at two games apiece. It seems a modest goal for a team that, not so long ago, spoke of outsize ambitions. But the Pacers are a problem, and so is James's supporting cast.

The first four games of the series have been a struggle for the many Cavaliers not named LeBron James. The group has, at times, looked close to buckling under the weight of expectations.

No one knows for certain what a premature postseason exit would mean for this team, but there would be fallout.

James, of course, could decline his player option and become a free agent. You may have heard this before. Cue the Cleveland agita.

The issue, or at least one of them, is that James has been playing to his usual all-universe standards against the Pacers — and Cleveland is still in trouble. So far in the series, James has averaged 32.5 points, 11.8 rebounds and 8 assists a game while shooting 54.1 percent from the field. The Cavaliers not named LeBron James are shooting 40.7 percent.

Korver provided some hope with his late-game shooting in Game 4, which helped nudge the Cavaliers to a 104-100 victory. But James had to play 46 minutes for them to even have a chance, and his workload at age 33 is equal parts mystifying, amazing and concerning. He appeared in all 82 games this season and led the league in minutes played.

"You feel like he just keeps getting better," Brett Brown, the coach of the Philadelphia 76ers, said before the start of the playoffs, adding, " I think he's playing arguably his best basketball."

Brown really likes James, who could — could — consider Philadelphia as a possible destination if he wants out of Cleveland, where he is both beloved and revered.

It would be hard to argue that James has ever been a more complete player — he set a career-high this season by averaging 9.1 assists a game — and a deep postseason run with this hodgepodge roster would be one of his most dazzling feats to date. It just seems so unlikely.

James used to have more help. He had Kyrie Irving — until Irving demanded a trade last summer. And back when he was with the Miami Heat, James shared the court with Dwyane Wade and Chris Bosh, a superfriends collective that won two N.B.A. championships. As his latest act, James has essentially gone solo. Not entirely by choice.

"There's a lot on his shoulders," Korver said. "But this is a team sport, and you've got to have everyone playing well. You've got to have everyone executing, and when we have our opportunities, we have to take advantage of them."

The organization spared James the ritual of answering reporters' questions after Tuesday's practice. He left those responsibilities to

Coach Tyronn Lue and a couple of teammates, who dusted off the usual postseason tropes about playing hard and playing together and how good it feels to play at home.

But Kevin Love has been laboring with a thumb injury. Tristan Thompson has been collecting dust at the end of the bench. George Hill is questionable for Game 5 with back spasms. And the Cavaliers, as a team, are shooting 32 percent from 3-point range. There is room for improvement.

The Pacers are testing the Cavaliers — punishing them, even. Yet Lue spun the series in the most positive way.

"I think it's good for us," he said.

Good for the Cavaliers if they manage to advance, that is. Even then, they seem to be tiptoeing down an uncertain path.

Only James knows where it leads.

LeBron James and
the Superstar Fallacy

OPINION | BY WILL LEITCH | MAY 19, 2018

LIKE MANY SPORTS FANS, I define eras of my own life by the sports super-stars who dominated them. In high school, it was Joe Montana; in college, Michael Jordan; post-college, Barry Bonds. Their career arcs become our story lines and plots that unfurl over many happy, occa-sionally anxious, years.

Today's biggest superstar is LeBron James, who's so big he can call the president "you bum" and barely get an angry tweet in response. James is the transcendent star of this era. Yet he is in trouble. It's all because of what I call the fallacy of the superstar.

James's Cleveland Cavaliers have fallen behind the Boston Celtics 2-0 in their Eastern Conference Finals matchup. This despite the fact that during the season, the Celtics lost their two best players, Kyrie Irving and Gordon Heyward, to injury. A loss in the series would be nearly unprecedented for James; in his past seven seasons, in both Cleveland and Miami, his teams reached an absurd seven consecu-tive N.B.A. finals. Three ended with James hoisting the Larry O'Brien championship trophy.

This one looks extremely dicey. Teams have gone down 2-0 in their series 300 times in N.B.A. history, and only 19 have come back to win them. (Further evidence of James's greatness: Two of them were his teams. Yes, he's that extraordinary.)

But James has perhaps less talent around him than he has had in a decade, and he's beginning to show the strain, visibly gasping at the end of long nights carrying the full load for his sagging team. If this is his last season in Cleveland, as many N.B.A. observers suspect, his "I'm Coming Home" tour will end in discord, exhaustion and defeat. It's red alert time.

What's strange, and unusually frustrating, about this is that LeBron James is having the best year of his career. James — who very well might be the best basketball player who has ever lived — has never been better than he is right now. He has scored 40 points five times this postseason, the highest of his career, one of which was also a triple double. He notched a career high in both average rebounds and assists this season, with his highest scoring average in eight years. He played all 82 games for the first time, and led the N.B.A. in minutes played per game for the second consecutive year. His Value Over Replacement Player, a statistic he is already the all-time leader in, was the highest in the N.B.A. this year, the first time he'd done that since 2013. This is peak LeBron.

But it sure doesn't feel that way right now, does it? For all the "Saturday Night Live" jokes about how James's teammates are anonymous extras in the saga that is LeBron — "our point guard is a Roomba!" — if the Cavaliers lose to the Celtics, no one will say "Kevin Love falls short." They'll say LeBron James did. In 10 years, you won't remember that Jordan Clarkson and Rodney Hood ever even played for the Cavaliers, but you'll remember the year that James couldn't keep his N.B.A. finals streak going. History has a way of remembering this as solely on the shoulders of the boldface name. This failure will be James's.

And that is the fallacy of the superstar, the tendency we have to frame team defeats as the fault of the best player rather than all the inferior teammates beside him, whose fault it (obviously) is in the first place. It's basic illogic, the tendency to focus on the front-facing star's mistakes rather than the countless more made by lesser players with obvious limitations. (It would be like blaming a star city reporter at a newspaper for a box score error in the sports section, or your brilliant physics professor for a declining graduation rate.) It won't be James's fault if the Cavaliers lose; it will be Jeff Green's, Larry Nance Jr.'s and George Hill's. Without James, this Cavaliers team would be one of the five worst in the N.B.A. With him, they're a step away from the finals.

I wonder if this, like so much about athletic superstar culture, can be traced back to Michael Jordan. He was an incredible player, obviously, but one of his most impressive skills was his ability to persuade everyone around him that his team's success was entirely a product of his own will and fortitude. Jordan's six championships were won alongside Hall of Famer Scottie Pippen (Dennis Rodman, another Hall of Famer, joined them for three), coached by the man who has won more N.B.A. titles than any coach in the history of the sport, and all coincided with Jordan's prime: When Jordan was at his best, his supporting cast was at its best. James's prime is giving him no such advantage; one shudders to think how Jordan would have reacted if he realized his only option was passing the ball to Jose Calderon. But because Jordan made us all believe that his titles were his and his alone, a Cavaliers' loss feels like a James loss.

The upside of this is the spoils; if the Cavaliers somehow come back from this deficit and defeat the Celtics, we'll all credit James solely. (And rightly.) But the boom-and-bust nature of watching sports, the beautiful simplicity of being happy when your team wins and sad when it loses, can't help landing unfairly on James's back anytime he doesn't pull off the impossible. If James's point guard actually were a Roomba, we'd all acknowledge it as a bit of a problem for him. But we'd still expect him to hit the winning shot … and we wouldn't blame the Roomba if he didn't. We'd blame him.

WILL LEITCH is a national correspondent for MLB.com, a contributing editor for New York magazine, a contributor to Sports Illustrated and the founder of Deadspin.

Why Kobe Bryant Fans Don't Like LeBron James

BY SCOTT CACCIOLA | JULY 13, 2018

LAS VEGAS — The Los Angeles Lakers recently acquired a high-profile player, but many longtime fans have been arriving here for N.B.A. Summer League paying homage to the past. They wear jerseys bearing the Nos. 8 and 24, which belonged to Kobe Bryant during his long and productive career and now hang from the rafters in Staples Center.

"He gave his heart for the love of the game," said Nathan Andrews, 31, who works for the water department in Needles, Calif.

Andrews was wearing a gold No. 24 jersey and sounded downright wistful as he reminisced about Bryant's former greatness. But what about the future? Andrews had to be excited, right? The Lakers are back, baby!

Andrews grimaced.

"I'm not a fan of LeBron," he said.

A strange phenomenon is playing out within a subsection of Lakerland, as hard-core fans of Bryant — the so-called Mamba Army who are historically predisposed to disliking LeBron James for various reasons — cope with a new and apparently uncomfortable reality: James, their longtime nemesis, is suddenly the face of the franchise.

In interviews with about a dozen fans wearing Bryant jerseys at summer league in recent days, they expressed a mix of emotions about the team's recent signing of James. Some were excited — the Lakers have been very bad at basketball for several seasons, and James is very good at it — but many more sounded confused and annoyed. James, the league's most dominant force, still has much to prove.

"I don't even know where to start," said Stephanie Serrano, a 35-year-old fan from San Clemente, Calif. "He's such a diva sometimes."

Serrano, who counts herself as a Kobe acolyte and was wearing the throwback jersey to prove it, noted how Bryant had spent his entire

Los Angeles Lakers fans watch an N.B.A. Summer League game against the Chicago Bulls in Las Vegas.

20-year career with the Lakers. James, on the other hand, has hop-scotched from team to team, she said, chasing rings. She questioned his loyalty.

"Don't get me wrong: He's good," she said as she pondered the seasons ahead. "Maybe I'll feel differently once he wins a championship for the Lakers."

To fans like Serrano, Bryant is one of the greatest Lakers ever — if not the greatest. He was an 18-time All-Star. He helped deliver five championships, including two without Shaquille O'Neal. He may have stumbled in the twilight of his career — he averaged 17.6 points while shooting a subterranean 35.8 percent from the field in his final season ahead of retirement in 2016 — but perhaps he was deserving of a gluttonous year on his way out. Or at least that was the view of Kobe stans — his most dedicated devotees, who, some may say, take their fandom too seriously.

"He was 100 percent pure Lakers," said Matt Sheldon, a 37-year-old fan from Las Vegas. "The best basketball player I've ever seen."

Sheldon, who works in sales, wore his No. 24 throwback to watch the Lakers at summer league on a recent evening. He got a little emotional when he talked about Bryant, referring to the "Mamba mentality" as if it were a guiding principle.

"The best," he said.

As for the team's most recent big-name acquisition? Sheldon made clear that his feelings toward James were more nuanced. He drew a sharp distinction between the James who played for the Cleveland Cavaliers and the Miami Heat — "He was a whiny baby," he said — and the James who recently signed with the Lakers.

"You put up points in a Lakers uniform, you're good with me," Sheldon said. "And he's going to put up a lot of points in a Lakers uniform."

He added, "It doesn't mean I need to hang out with him."

Other hard-core, jersey-wearing fans of Bryant were not quite so ready to move on from the James of yore. Jeremy Gonzales, a 20-year-old student from Long Beach, Calif., rattled through a list of criticisms, including his allegation that James is a lazy defender. (James has been named to the league's all-defensive team six times.)

"I also didn't like that he didn't want to shoot," Gonzales said. "And now that he shoots, I still don't like that he doesn't have a post game."

All that being said, Gonzales recalled the moment he received the news alert on his phone that James had agreed to join the Lakers.

"Oh," he said, "I was hyped."

Two fans who were decidedly not hyped by the signing were Janessa Yumul, 28, and Jessica Dawana, 29, longtime friends from Southern California who color coordinated their Bryant jerseys for summer league: Yumul in yellow, Dawana in white.

"Lake show for life!" said Dawana, who works in human resources technology.

Yumul and Dawana said they had revered Bryant since the start of his career, citing his toughness and competitive fire. They do not love James. Not yet, anyway.

"I never liked him," said Yumul, an ultrasound technician who now lives in Las Vegas. "I always thought he seemed really cocky."

"And dramatic," Dawana said.

To illustrate what she described as the difference between the two players, Dawana recalled how Bryant once sank two free throws after tearing his Achilles' tendon.

"Who does that?" she said. "Whereas with LeBron it's like, 'Ehhhhh!' "

As she said this, Dawana fell backward as if to suggest that James tumbles over in stiff breezes or suffers from fainting spells.

Dawana added that she was worried the addition of James would upset the development of an "up-and-coming team," which finished last season with a 35-47 record. But Dawana said she would try her hardest to enter this new era, featuring the greatest player on the planet, with an open mind. After all, Bryant had given the move his blessing via Twitter.

"But I'm not excited about it," she said.

Mychal Thompson, a former power forward who won two championships with the "Showtime"-era Lakers of the late 1980s, said he understood why so many fans still hold Bryant in such high regard.

"Oh, that's easy, man: his passion, his competitiveness and his desire to win," Thompson said in a telephone interview. "He gave fans every ounce he had. Kobe would never take a night off. And if you asked him if he wanted to rest, he would look at you like you're crazy."

Thompson was less understanding about the anti-LeBron sentiment in at least one corner of the Lakers fan base. That segment, Thompson said, seems to be afraid that James is supplanting Bryant on the list of all-time greats — assuming, of course, that he has not already. Many fans want to preserve Bryant's legacy as much as possible.

Glenn Gagan, 25, who traveled to summer league from his home in Winnipeg, Manitoba, said he did not like James — right up until the minute he signed with the Lakers, and then everything changed. Gagan said he waited five hours at an outlet mall to buy a James jersey in purple and gold.

"I'm excited," he said. "It's been a long time coming for Lakers fans."

A long time coming, perhaps, but rocky on the landing for Kobe fans who aren't ready to let go of what was.

Gagan isn't one of them.

While he proudly sported his new James jersey around summer league, he didn't feel the need to wear his No. 24 underneath or have it clutched in his hands, though he kept it close. He had given that jersey away, to his girlfriend.

LeBron James Is Hurt in Lakers' Blowout of the Warriors

BY SCOTT CACCIOLA | DEC. 25, 2018

OAKLAND, CALIF. — The Los Angeles Lakers defeated the Golden State Warriors on Tuesday night, but lost LeBron James — at least for the time being.

After leading the Lakers to a sizable lead, James left the game in the third quarter with what the team described as a strained left groin. He did not return, but the Lakers had no trouble pulverizing the Warriors without him, rolling to a 127-101 victory, their first win at Oracle Arena since December 2012.

There was obvious cause for concern for the Lakers not only because James is one of the greatest players of his generation but also because he is one of its most durable. Coach Luke Walton said James would undergo a magnetic resonance imaging exam on Wednesday to determine the extent of the injury; Walton did not offer a timetable for his return.

"Just overextended my groin, I guess," said James, who did not rule out playing on Thursday against the Sacramento Kings. "It's unfortunate."

Now in his 16th season, James has never sustained a serious injury. Last season, he appeared in all 82 games for the Cleveland Cavaliers. And the only season during which he missed more than 10 games was 2014-15, when he struggled with back issues. He rounded into shape in time to lead the Cavaliers to the N.B.A. finals.

After Tuesday's game, James said he "takes a lot of pride" in not missing games because of injuries.

"That's why it pissed me off not being able to go back into the game," he said. "More than anything, being available to my teammates, being available to my coaching staff — that's something that I take more personal than anything. So hopefully it's not a long thing, and I can get back on the floor as soon as possible."

The Lakers were leading by 71-57 on Tuesday when James left the game, thanks in part to his 17 points, 13 rebounds and 5 assists in 21 minutes.

It was looking like one of James's vintage Christmas Day performances until he caught himself under one of the baskets with 7 minutes 51 seconds left in the third quarter, wincing in pain. Walton called for a timeout.

Lakers trainers met James on the court as he tried to do some stretching, and he could be heard telling them that he felt something "pop." He soon left for the locker room.

"Obviously, we want him back as soon as possible," Walton said. "But we also will be very cautious with when we bring him back."

Without James, his younger teammates showed plenty of resilience against the defending champions. After the Warriors (23-12) initially cut into their lead with James off the court, the Lakers (20-14) responded to build it up again by attacking the basket and stifling the Warriors along the perimeter.

Kyle Kuzma led the Lakers with 19 points, but it was a balanced effort. Ivica Zubac had 18 points, Rajon Rondo had 15, and Brandon Ingram added 14. The Warriors shot just 40.9 percent from the field.

There Are Lakers Not Named LeBron James — and They Are Not So Bad

BY SCOTT CACCIOLA | DEC. 26, 2018

OAKLAND, CALIF. — It did not seem confrontational, and he did not sound upset. But Kyle Kuzma wanted to make his feelings known.

"I mean, it's not like we're panicking because he's gone," Kuzma, the second-year forward with the Los Angeles Lakers, said late Tuesday night. "We're pros, too. We're great players — or on our way to trying to be great players. So it's all about that next-up mentality and having a will to win."

Kuzma was speaking with reporters in the visiting locker room at Oracle Arena not long after the Lakers had demolished the Golden State Warriors, 127-101, on Christmas Day, and the "he" to whom Kuzma was referring was LeBron James, the leader of the Lakers and the most dominant player of his generation.

James had strained his left groin in the third quarter, leaving his teammates to fend for themselves against the N.B.A.'s reigning champions. The training wheels were off, and the Lakers' lesser lights seized the opportunity.

In his own way, Kuzma appeared to be alluding to a lesson — that it is no easy thing to labor in James's shadow — that all of James's teammates eventually learn. And with that lesson often comes a resolve: to show that the other members of the team have some pride and skills, and are capable of at least approximating a competitive basketball team in James's absence.

For one night, the Lakers (20-14) proved as much — and they may have more opportunities ahead, starting Thursday against Sacramento.

The Lakers announced Wednesday that James would not travel with the team to play the Kings and that his status was day-to-day after a magnetic resonance imaging test confirmed that the groin had only been strained, and not more seriously damaged.

Shortly before the announcement, James posted on Twitter: "Dodged a bullet! Sheesh" and "#BackInNoTime."

"It's uncharted territory, obviously, with this group," Lakers Coach Luke Walton said Tuesday night, before the extent of the injury was known, "but this is what we've been talking about, and this is what we've tried to play for — not that he gets hurt, but being able to play and win and compete while he's not on the floor. That's progress, and our team is much better now than we were to start out the season."

James played in all 82 games last season with the Cleveland Cavaliers — but he will turn 34 on Sunday.

The injury news comes during a stretch in which James has attracted different, if not more, attention than usual. Last week, in response to a question, he said he would love for Anthony Davis of the New Orleans Pelicans to join him in Los Angeles. Alvin Gentry, the coach of the Pelicans, then accused James of tampering with a player under contract, but the N.B.A. determined that James had not violated league policy. Gentry later defended the Lakers star, saying he had been put in a "bad situation" when he was initially asked about Davis.

In either case, James was broadcasting the idea that he was open to upgrading the talent around him — and, in fairness, who wouldn't want to play with an all-world talent like Davis? But the math goes something like this: One or more of the current Lakers would need to go to New Orleans in a trade for Davis, which must mean that James thinks they are expendable.

A few days later, James made the rare public misstep of posting offensive lyrics on his Instagram account. He subsequently apologized in an interview with ESPN — "if I offended anyone," he said. The lyrics, by the rapper 21 Savage, include the phrase "getting that Jewish money," and James said: "I actually thought it was a compliment, and obviously it wasn't through the lens of a lot of people."

Amid that situation, the latest episode of James's H.B.O. show "The Shop" aired. In it, James described N.F.L. owners as "old white men" with a "slave mentality."

By Tuesday night, though, the focus was back on LeBron James the basketball player. He was brilliant, collecting 17 points, 13 rebounds and 5 assists as he led the Lakers to a 14-point advantage over Golden State early in the third quarter. But after lunging for a loose ball, James felt some discomfort in his groin, he said, and he may have aggravated the injury when he tried to make a defensive play. He soon left for the locker room.

"I've never seen him hurt," Lakers guard Rajon Rondo said.

The Warriors rallied, cutting the lead to 2 late in the third quarter. But then something unexpected happened: The Lakers pulled away behind players like Rondo (15 points, 10 assists), Kuzma (19 points, 6 rebounds), Brandon Ingram (14 points) and Ivica Zubac, a 21-year-old center who finished with 18 points and 11 rebounds while shooting 9 of 10 from the field.

Zubac has gotten an opportunity only in recent days, because JaVale McGee, the team's starting center, has been sidelined by an illness. Zubac had barely been playing.

"It's tough, especially mentally — it's the worst," Zubac said. "Everyone's saying: 'You've got to stay ready. You've got to stay ready.' And you know you can play, but there are a lot of guys ahead of you in the rotation, so you have to wait until someone goes down, and that's your only chance. And you've got to step up. If you don't step up at that time, you're not playing, like, for the next 20 games."

Zubac has channeled that sense of urgency into incredible production, averaging 17.7 points and 8.7 rebounds while shooting 78.1 percent from the field in his last three games — and perhaps the rest of the team will look to him as an example if James is out for a while.

"He's a big part of us, obviously," Kuzma said of James. "He makes us go. But that's why it's a team sport."

CHAPTER 4

On the Political Court

LeBron James is outspoken about what he believes in, including politics. He endorsed Hillary Clinton in the 2016 presidential election and has stood up to racist comments. LeBron James is in the spotlight during a time when athletes in both the N.F.L. and the N.B.A. are taking a stand against racism. It is a time characterized by debates, protests and activism, many on the topic of what it means to be black in the United States.

Burden Unites the Cleveland Stars Jim Brown and LeBron James

BY WILLIAM C. RHODEN | JUNE 9, 2015

ON DEC. 27, 1964, Jim Brown asked the Cleveland Browns' coaches to leave the team's locker room. Brown had something he wanted to say to his teammates before they all took the field against the favored Baltimore Colts in the N.F.L. championship game.

Brown said he had never done this before.

While he was the greatest running back of his or anyone else's generation and the acknowledged leader of the team, he preferred to let his play provide the inspiration. But this was a special moment at the end of what had been yet another harrowing year of civil rights struggles in the United States.

"In order to win that game," Brown recalled Monday, "we had to be conscious of what was at stake."

So, in his deep voice, he told his teammates that they needed to put everything aside — race, politics, anything — and focus only on one another and the task at hand.

"And that's what we did," he said.

The Browns won, 27-0, in one of the bigger upsets in N.F.L. championship history.

Fifty-one years after Brown led Cleveland to a major championship, LeBron James is attempting to carry the Cleveland Cavaliers to the city's next one. And like Brown, James and his team are the underdogs.

The Golden State Warriors, like the 1964 Colts, have a high-octane offense. They also have a dazzling pair of All-Stars in Stephen Curry and Klay Thompson. The undermanned Cavaliers have James and a crew of workmanlike players determinedly following his lead, all of them trying to compensate in these N.B.A. finals for the absence of two Cleveland stars — Kyrie Irving and Kevin Love.

For that reason, Brown's task in 1964 seems a little easier than the one James faces now. James's group, defying the odds, turned back Golden State in Games 2 and 3 to give Cleveland a two-games-to-one series lead, when few people were giving them much of a chance to actually take four games against the Warriors and win the N.B.A. title. Still, to have any shot, James, who had 40 points, 12 rebounds and 8 assists in the Cavaliers' 96-91 win Tuesday night, will do well to keep to Brown's blueprint.

"We had to go into that rarefied area," Brown said, recalling 1964. "Sometimes, a superstar can't go there, so when you're talking to ordinary players, you've got to let them know that they're going to be called upon to go somewhere they've never been."

James, of course, has already won two championships, but that was in Miami, with two star players, Dwyane Wade and Chris Bosh, at his side. Now he has J. R. Smith and Matthew Dellavedova and Iman Shumpert. Some talent, yes. Stars, no.

Brown, who has criticized a number of contemporary sports stars, said without hesitation that he was a LeBron James fan. In fact, he attended Tuesday night's game to support James, who is as much the King in Cleveland today as Brown was in 1964.

Just as many Cleveland players learned this season what it's like to play with a once-in-a-career talent like James, the former Browns receiver Paul Warfield said he had no idea what it meant to play with a superstar until he played with Brown.

Warfield, a rookie in 1964, said the championship game against Baltimore — indeed, the entire season — had been one surreal moment after another. A product of Warren, Ohio, and a star at Ohio State, Warfield had grown up a Browns fan, and a Jim Brown devotee.

"The entire intent of any defensive football team and opponent that we played against, the emphasis was not to stop me or stop my teammate Gary Collins," Warfield said. "The sole intent of the defensive unit, whoever we played against, was dedicated 110 percent on every play to stopping Jim Brown. And still they couldn't stop him."

Opponents treat James with the same respect, gearing entire defenses to rotate toward James whenever he has the ball, and accounting for his every move when he does not.

And just as the obsession with Brown created opportunities for Warfield and Collins, the obsession with James makes it possible for role players to flourish.

By the time the Browns met the Colts in the 1964 championship game in Cleveland, teams had been forced to shift at least a little of the focus away from stopping Brown to figuring out ways to clamp down on Warfield. That left the other wide receiver, Collins, with single coverage. In the championship game, Collins scored three touchdowns.

Afterward, Brown, who never gushed and rarely showed animated exuberance, recalled growing emotional as he congratulated his teammates.

"My inner satisfaction was tremendous, but it was something I don't share too often," he said. "But on that victory stand, it was a great, great feeling as a football player, and also as a man."

Cleveland today is a different place from what it was in 1964. I asked Brown if he thought being the city's biggest sports star was more challenging for him than it is for James in 2015.

"The circumstances are different," he said, "but they are not as different as they should be."

In the Brown mold, James, at 30, has emerged as a leader off the court as he has matured as a player. He was vocal in calling for the removal of the Los Angeles Clippers owner Donald Sterling last year. He wore an "I Can't Breathe" T-shirt to protest acts of police violence, and last month, he called for calm when a white Cleveland policeman was acquitted in the shooting deaths of two black motorists.

"In a subtler way, he has had to carry the same kind of burden and use the same kind of wisdom," Brown said. "For him to have to have the ability to deal with the politics of being back in Cleveland, dealing with the politics of his own team, I have great admiration for what I see as a great contribution by a human being on and off the field."

In Brown's Cleveland, there was segregation and discrimination. There is segregation, too, in James's Cleveland, but blacks with wealth — like James — are able to navigate around some forms of racism.

In the end, James and Brown are separated by age and their sports but connected by Cleveland and by a real understanding of the role leadership plays in championship moments.

Scoring touchdowns was not the only source of Brown's greatness, nor are points the sole source for James's. What Brown did, and what James is now trying to do, is inspire those around them to reach higher than they thought possible.

"The way he expresses himself, the way that he plays, and the understanding that he has of what his role is, is very refreshing," Brown said of James. "It's rare for a man that young to have that kind of wisdom."

LeBron James, Calling for Hope and Unity, Endorses Hillary Clinton

BY YAMICHE ALCINDOR | OCT. 2, 2016

LEBRON JAMES, WHO last season led the Cleveland Cavaliers to their first N.B.A. championship, endorsed Hillary Clinton for president on Sunday.

Mr. James announced his decision in an op-ed article in Business Insider, saying that Mrs. Clinton understands the struggles of childhood poverty and as president would enact policies that would build on the legacy of President Obama.

He also said he believed Mrs. Clinton would champion causes for children, provide more educational opportunities and "address the violence, of every kind, the African-American community is experiencing."

"Only one person running truly understands the struggles of an Akron child born into poverty," wrote Mr. James, who grew up in Akron and who praised his own foundation's efforts to help at-risk young people. "And when I think about the kinds of policies and ideas the kids in my foundation need from our government, the choice is clear. That candidate is Hillary Clinton."

Mr. James is popular across the country and particularly in Ohio, but it is unclear how much his endorsement of Mrs. Clinton will influence the race with her opponent Donald J. Trump.

Most recent surveys show Mr. Trump with a slight edge among voters in Ohio. A Suffolk University poll from September put him at 42 percent, compared to 39 percent for Mrs. Clinton. His double-digit leads among men and white voters are crucial to his standing in the state.

Mr. James, who has been outspoken about recent police killings of black men and women, wrote that Mrs. Clinton would seek to improve life for African-Americans.

"Finally, we must address the violence, of every kind, the African-American community is experiencing in our streets and seeing on our

TVs," he wrote. "However, I am not a politician, I don't know every-thing it will take finally to end the violence. But I do know we need a president who brings us together and keeps us unified."

"Policies and ideas that divide us more are not the solution," he continued. "We must all stand together — no matter where we are from or the color of our skin. And Hillary is running on the message of hope and unity that we need."

Mr. James is one of several athletes who have weighed in on the presidential race.

The golfer John Daly, the former football star Herschel Walker and the former basketball coach Bob Knight have endorsed Mr. Trump, according to Sports Illustrated. The magazine also said that the for-mer professional wrestler Hulk Hogan and the former N.B.A. player Dennis Rodman have expressed support for Mr. Trump.

LeBron James Fires Back at Phil Jackson for 'Posse' Comment

BY MIKE VORKUNOV | NOV. 15, 2016

PHIL JACKSON'S DESCRIPTION of LeBron James's business partners as his "posse" in an interview published by ESPN on Monday drew an angry response from James, who took offense at the racial connotation of the word.

The dispute between Jackson, the Knicks' president, and James, who plays for the Cleveland Cavaliers and is one of the N.B.A.'s most visible players, also left Knicks forward Carmelo Anthony in the uncomfortable position of having to answer questions about a sudden feud involving one of his bosses and one of his good friends.

The ESPN interview was a wide-ranging Q. and A. in which Jackson talked about the state of the Knicks, the criticism of his management of the team, and his relationship with Anthony. But James took exception with Jackson's description of the group of friends who travel and work with him as his "posse."

James and Maverick Carter, his close friend and business partner, both took offense at Jackson's use of the word. Carter told ESPN.com he was bothered because of the idea that Jackson said it because James and his friends are "young and black, he can use that word." James said he had lost respect for Jackson as a result of the comments.

"We see the success that we have, but then there is always someone that lets you know how far we still have to go as African-Americans," James told reporters in Cleveland. "I don't believe that Phil Jackson would have used that term if he was doing business with someone else and working with another team or if he was working with anybody in sports that was owning a team that wasn't African-American and had a group of guys around them that didn't agree with what they did. I don't think he would have called them a posse. But it just shows how far we have to go. But it won't stop us from doing what we need to do as a group."

James, Carter and two other high school friends, Rich Paul and Randy Mims, founded L.R.M.R. Management Company a decade ago. The agency handles marketing and representation duties for James and other N.B.A. players. The company has been successful since its inception, positioning James as one of the top athletes-turned-entrepreneurs of his generation.

In the ESPN interview, Jackson, responding to a question about James's decision to leave the Miami Heat, and whether he could imagine Magic Johnson leaving Pat Riley and the Los Angeles Lakers or Michael Jordan leaving Jackson and the Chicago Bulls, turned his response back around to James.

"When LeBron was playing with the Heat, they went to Cleveland and he wanted to spend the night," Jackson told ESPN.com. "They don't do overnights. Teams just don't. So now Spoelstra" — a reference to the Heat coach, Erik Spoelstra — "has to text Riley and say, 'What do I do in this situation?' And Pat, who has iron-fist rules, answers, 'You are on the plane, you are with this team.' You can't hold up the whole team because you and your mom and your posse want to spend an extra night in Cleveland."

Jackson did not respond to James's remarks Tuesday; he left Knicks practice without speaking to members of the news media and did not respond to an email.

While posse is defined as a group of friends or associates, Keith Gilyard, a professor of English and African-American studies at Penn State, said he could understand why James took offense. The cultural definition of the word has shifted toward defining drug cartels or, in cultural terms, the group of hangers-on that surround a celebrity.

"What we're talking about is a rhetorical moment, and one of the things that's interesting about rhetoric is sort of the study of who can say what to whom and under what conditions — or can say what about whom and under what conditions," Gilyard said. "The word in and of itself is never neutral. It never means the same in all contexts."

And when the word is used publicly, as by Jackson, instead of in a private conversation, its connotation changes, Gilyard said.

"When you have an official or executive that uses that language that makes its way into mainstream circulation, it has a different meaning," he added. "Meaning shifts depending on contexts."

With Jackson unavailable, it left Anthony, a close friend of James's, to answer questions about the subject. Anthony agreed that he considered "posse" a loaded term, and he said that he would not want his group of friends or family to be referred that way. But Anthony declined to ascribe any assumptions or intent to Jackson.

"Do I think he meant it any kind of way?" Anthony said. "I really don't know. I don't think he did. I would hope that he didn't.

"Sometimes Phil just says things and he says the first thing that comes to mind and then probably is in his office right now regretting it. I don't know. When it comes to Phil, you just never know what's going to be said, what's coming out. It depends on who's listening. People take it the right way or people take it the wrong way. You just never know when it comes to Phil.

"I just don't understand him talking about LeBron right now, in November. I don't understand that."

LeBron James Boycotts Donald Trump's Hotel, Then Beats Up Knicks

BY SCOTT CACCIOLA | DEC. 7, 2016

LEBRON JAMES HAS DONE a lot and seen a lot over the course of his 14-year N.B.A. career. He has won championships. He has traveled the globe. He has become an icon in his chosen field.

But James is still finding ways to mark out new territory. Such was the case this week when, for the first time in his career, he opted not to stay at his team's designated hotel, ahead of the Cleveland Cavaliers' 126-94 victory over the Knicks on Wednesday night at Madison Square Garden.

The team hotel, in this instance, was the Trump SoHo. A number of James's teammates joined him at a different (and undisclosed) Manhattan hotel in what amounted to a modest political protest.

Nevertheless, James insisted he was not "trying to make a statement," telling reporters at the team's Wednesday morning practice at the Garden that his decision to stay at a hotel not bearing Donald J. Trump's name was "just my personal preference."

"At the end of the day, I hope he's one of the best presidents ever for all of our sake — for my family, for all of us," James said of Trump, the president-elect. "But just my personal preference. It would be the same if I went to a restaurant and decided to eat chicken and not steak."

It was hardly a forceful statement from James, who endorsed Hillary Clinton during the presidential campaign and made a public appearance with her shortly before the election. And James was not eager to elaborate, cutting off a reporter who wanted to ask more about Trump.

"Next question, please," James said.

Perhaps his choice to stay elsewhere was enough — enough to convey displeasure with Trump and some of his rhetoric and enough to reinforce James's own status within the N.B.A. when it comes to social issues.

LeBron James said his decision not to stay at a hotel bearing the name of President-elect Donald J. Trump was "just my personal preference."

In a league in which players and coaches have become increasingly outspoken, and in which the commissioner, Adam Silver, seems fine with just about all of it, James can still be cautious with his words. But he is opinionated when he wants to be, and at age 31, with three championships to his name, he seems more self-assured than ever.

Consider his response when he was asked what he had learned about himself since winning a championship with Cleveland last season.

Nothing, was his answer.

"I know who I am, and I know what I'm capable of," he said.

That clearly seems to be the case. And his visit to New York, his first this season, was particularly unusual in that it was not just Trump whom James, in some sense, was taking on.

He is now in a protracted standoff with Phil Jackson, the president of the Knicks and the man with more championships (11) than any other coach in N.B.A. history.

Jackson ran afoul of James last month for describing James's business partners as a "posse" in an interview with ESPN. James said that he considered the word to be racially charged and that, as a result, he had lost respect for Jackson. Even before arriving in New York, James said he had no interest in meeting with Jackson to clear the air.

And that was that, as far as James was concerned. "I'm not answering any Phil Jackson questions," he told reporters at the practice.

There is basketball to consider, too, of course. James and his Cavaliers teammates arrived in New York, if not at the Trump SoHo, on the heels of a 116-112 victory over the Toronto Raptors that halted a three-game losing streak, a rare stretch of adversity for these defending champions.

And in roasting the Knicks, the Cavaliers improved their record to 15-5, the best mark in the Eastern Conference. With Jackson watching from his usual perch several rows into the crowd, James was dynamic, collecting 25 points, 7 assists and 6 rebounds. He soared for dunks, turned defenders into traffic cones and elicited gasps from the crowd.

James directing the offense during their 126-94 victory over the Knicks.

"It's always special," he said before the game of playing at the Garden. "There's so much history in this building, so many performers — not just in sports but in general. So it's always great to be an outsider coming in here."

As to which Cavaliers joined James in staying at a different hotel, and which did not, a team spokesman would say only that "a good number" boycotted the Trump SoHo, where the team had booked rooms well ahead of the current season and the presidential election. (While the hotel bears Trump's name, he is no longer an owner.)

One of those who did not stay elsewhere, however, was James's coach, Tyronn Lue.

"I mean, it's not normal," Lue said at the practice when asked about the two-hotel arrangement. "But considering the circumstances, that's what we have. That's not my main objective. My main thing is to try to get this team to stay on track and play the right way."

James and the teammates who joined him at the second hotel are not the first athletes to take this sort of step to dissociate themselves from Trump.

First baseman Adrian Gonzalez opted not to stay with his Los Angeles Dodgers teammates at a Trump hotel in Chicago in May. And last month, ESPN reported that three N.B.A. teams — the Milwaukee Bucks, the Memphis Grizzlies and the Dallas Mavericks — were no longer staying at Trump-brand properties in New York and Chicago.

A press officer for Trump declined to comment.

For James and the Cavaliers, there was Plan B: two hotels for one team. Still, James said the Cavaliers took only one bus to the Garden for the practice, where his teammates, as usual, fell in line behind him. It was more of the same.

LeBron James Responds to Racial Vandalism: 'Being Black in America Is Tough'

BY SCOTT CACCIOLA AND JONAH ENGEL BROMWICH | MAY 31, 2017

OAKLAND, CALIF. — As he has grown older, and as he has established himself as one of the great athletes in American history, LeBron James has become increasingly willing to address social and political issues. He has, for instance, denounced police killings of African-American men, and he took sides in the 2016 presidential campaign, endorsing Hillary Clinton and making a public appearance on her behalf.

The pointed and difficult topics that often grip this country have become familiar terrain for James. But on the eve of his seventh straight trip to the N.B.A. finals, James was, by his own admission, distracted and upset, his mind wandering from the supreme challenge that he and the Cleveland Cavaliers again face in taking on the Golden State Warriors with everything at stake.

The series begins on Thursday night, but on Wednesday afternoon, as James addressed a group of reporters on hand to cover Game 1, he said that all he wanted at that moment was to be with his children.

"This is kind of killing me inside right now," he said. The "this" James was referring to was that he was not at home to comfort his children over the racial slur that, the police said Wednesday, was painted on the front gates of a Los Angeles-area home that James owns.

Several hours after the episode was disclosed, James discussed it at what became a frank and emotional news conference in Oakland at Oracle Arena, the home of the Warriors. James said the vandalism illustrated the difficulties black people faced in America.

"No matter how much money you have, no matter how famous you are, no matter how many people admire you, being black in America is — it's tough," James said. "And we got a long way to go for us as a society and for us as African-Americans until we feel equal in America."

Officer Norma Eisenman, a spokeswoman for the Los Angeles Police Department, said that the act of vandalism at James's home was being investigated as a hate crime and that the slur had been painted over by the property's managers. The Plain Dealer of Cleveland reported that James's wife and three children were at the family's home in Bath Township, Ohio, at the time of the episode.

"My family is safe," James said, adding: "Obviously, you see I'm not my normal energetic self. It will pass. That's fine. I'm figuring it out. I'm thinking about my kids a lot."

If nothing else, James said, he saw the episode as another opportunity to address an issue that is important to him.

"If this incident that happened to me and my family today can keep the conversation going and can shed light on us trying to figure out a way to keep progressing and not regressing, then I'm not against it happening to us again," he said. "I mean, it's as long as my family is safe."

Over the last several seasons, James has used his platform as the league's most visible superstar to voice opinions on matters that do not necessarily involve what he does on the court. His increasing willingness to speak his mind has set him apart from stars of previous eras, including Michael Jordan, to whom he is often compared as a player.

James, a four-time N.B.A. most valuable player, won the league's annual J. Walter Kennedy Citizenship Award last month in connection with his efforts to improve educational opportunities in his hometown, Akron, Ohio.

On the court, of course, James remains as fearsome as ever. Through the first three rounds of this year's playoffs, he averaged 32.5 points, 8 rebounds and 7 assists per game while shooting 56.6 percent from the field. Now he confronts the Warriors, again, after losing to them in the finals in 2015 and then stunning them last year to give the Cavaliers their first N.B.A. title.

"I will be as focused as I can be on the job at hand tomorrow," James said Wednesday. "But this is a situation where it just puts me back in place of what's actually more important, and basketball's not the most important thing in my life."

The appearance of the slur on James's home, in West Los Angeles, was reported at 6:44 a.m. Wednesday, said Officer Aereon Jefferson, a spokesman for the Police Department. He said it had been painted over by the property's managers by the time that officers arrived a short while later.

Jefferson said that the episode was still being investigated and that the police did not know who first reported the slur.

At one point during Wednesday's news conference, James said that when he learned of the slur, he thought about the mother of Emmett Till. After her 14-year-old son was lynched in 1955, she insisted there be an open coffin so people could see for themselves the brutality of the murder.

"She wanted to show the world what her son went through as far as a hate crime and being black in America," James said.

So on a day when James might normally have been talking about the star players he will be battling on the Warriors, he was instead citing one of the more infamous moments in American history. However familiar Thursday night will be when the Warriors and the Cavaliers finally play Game 1, and James takes on Stephen Curry and Company, Wednesday ended up having a far different feel.

SCOTT CACCIOLA reported from Oakland, and JONAH ENGEL BROMWICH from New York.

'To Me, It Was Racist': N.B.A. Players Respond to Laura Ingraham's Comments on LeBron James

BY JONAH ENGEL BROMWICH | FEB. 16, 2018

THE FOX NEWS HOST Laura Ingraham on Thursday insulted LeBron James's intelligence and said he and his fellow basketball star Kevin Durant should not express their political opinions, comments that drew a strong rebuke from Mr. James, Mr. Durant, and the Miami Heat's Dwyane Wade.

Ms. Ingraham called recent statements Mr. James had made about President Trump "barely intelligible" in a segment on her Fox News show, "The Ingraham Angle."

Then, after showing a clip featuring Mr. James speaking about the president with Mr. Durant and the ESPN host Cari Champion, Ms. Ingraham asked, "Must they run their mouths like that?"

"You're great players but no one voted for you," she said, addressing Mr. James and Mr. Durant. "Millions elected Trump to be their coach. So keep the political commentary to yourself, or as someone once said, shut up and dribble."

At a news conference on Saturday, Mr. James addressed Ms. Ingraham's comments. "We're back to everything I've been talking over the past few years," he said. "It lets me know that everything I've been saying is correct, for her to have that type of reaction."

He added, "But we will definitely not shut up and dribble."

And in an interview with USA Today, Mr. Durant said Ms. Ingraham's segment was biased. "Ignorance is something I try to ignore. That was definitely an ignorant comment," he told USA Today. "To me, it was racist."

Mr. Wade, in a tweet, said that Ms. Ingraham's remarks underscored the way that racist speech has flourished under Mr. Trump.

"They use to try and hide it," said Mr. Wade, a close friend and former teammate of Mr. James. "Now the president has given everyone the courage to live their truths."

Ms. Ingraham's comments referred to a clip from Mr. James's video platform, Uninterrupted, in which Mr. James and Mr. Durant criticized the president. Mr. James spoke about his experience as an African-American and repeated his past criticisms of Mr. Trump.

Mr. Durant then described how he learned life skills from basketball and compared Mr. Trump to a "bad coach." On her show, Ms. Ingraham edited the clip to remove substantial portions of both men's comments.

Mr. James, Mr. Durant and Ms. Champion are black, and many commentators noted online that Ms. Ingraham's use of the word "they," and her comments about Mr. James's intelligence, came across as racist.

"If pro athletes and entertainers want to freelance as political pundits, then they should not be surprised when they're called out for insulting politicians," Ms. Ingraham said in a statement on Friday. "There was no racial intent in my remarks — false, defamatory charges of racism are a transparent attempt to immunize entertainment and sports elites from scrutiny and criticism." She also cited multiple white entertainers whom she had previously criticized for being politically outspoken.

Ms. Ingraham made similar arguments on Friday night's episode of her Fox News show before doubling down against Mr. James. "If you want to be a political pundit, you're coming on my court," she said.

She said she would welcome a conversation about black unemployment, inner-city violence and school choice, but that Mr. James's comments about Mr. Trump were a "drive-by hit."

"If you're a white N.B.A. player and you said that stuff about Obama, you would never play again," she said.

Mr. James has been politically outspoken, particularly in regard to Mr. Trump. In September, he called the president a "bum" after Mr. Trump said he had withdrawn an invitation for the Golden State Warriors to visit the White House.

After a racial slur was painted on the front gates of his home in Los Angeles last year, Mr. James addressed how he continues to struggle with racism, despite his success.

"No matter how much money you have, no matter how famous you are, no matter how many people admire you, being black in America is — it's tough," Mr. James said at the time. "And we got a long way to go for us as a society and for us as African-Americans until we feel equal in America."

JASON M. BAILEY contributed reporting.

LeBron James and Stephen Curry Unite Against White House Visits

BY BENJAMIN HOFFMAN | JUNE 5, 2018

PRESIDENT TRUMP NIXED the Philadelphia Eagles' White House victory ceremony at the last minute. He won't even have to bother inviting this year's N.B.A. champions.

In a display of solidarity between two of the game's fiercest rivals, Cleveland's LeBron James and Golden State's Stephen Curry — despite currently facing each other in an unprecedented fourth consecutive N.B.A. finals — each took time while speaking to the news media on Tuesday to make it clear that their teams would not participate in any sort of ceremony at the White House.

The visits are a long-held tradition for the league's champions, with President Kennedy having greeted the Boston Celtics as far back as 1963, and the Cavaliers having visited with President Obama as recently as November 2016.

"I know whoever wins this series, no one wants an invite," said James, whose Cavaliers are down, 2-0, in the best-of-seven series. Game 3 is scheduled for Wednesday night in Cleveland.

Curry, whose opposition to a visit after winning the championship last year was cited by President Trump in his public disinvitation of the team in September, agreed with James, saying that nothing had changed as far as he was concerned. But he added that he felt the decision should be left up to individual teams.

"Every team has an opportunity to make a decision for themselves and speak for themselves," he said. "I think that's powerful, being in this situation."

The topic returned to the forefront after the White House accused the N.F.L.'s Eagles of politicizing their visit by planning to send so few players; fewer than 10 members of the team were expected to attend the event scheduled for Tuesday. Instead of the Eagles celebration, Mr. Trump held a ceremony honoring the military.

James expressed disappointment that the situation was taking away from the Eagles' accomplishment of winning the Super Bowl.

Winning a championship in any sport, he said, "is way bigger than getting invited to the White House, especially with him in there, in my opinion."

White House visits by sports teams have historically been non-political celebrations, but they have been infused with political messaging under the Trump administration, with several prominent athletes in various sports expressing unease about participating. The situation created an alliance of sorts between James and Curry after James's public support of Curry in the wake of a tweet by the president last year that said: "Going to the White House is considered a great honor for a championship team. Stephen Curry is hesitating, therefore invitation is withdrawn!"

Less than three hours later, James issued a response to the president:

U bum @StephenCurry30 already said he ain't going! So therefore ain't no invite. Going to White House was a great honor until you showed up!

— LeBron James (@KingJames) Sep. 23, 2017

On the same weekend he rescinded the invitation to the Warriors, President Trump had also made comments at a political rally suggesting that N.F.L. players who protested during the national anthem should be fired. That statement led to widespread protests throughout the N.F.L., with hundreds of players demonstrating during the anthem, rather than the handful that had been doing so up until that point.

The N.F.L. recently adopted a policy in which players would be allowed to remain in the locker room during the anthem but would be required to stand if they were on the field. The N.B.A., by contrast, requires its players by rule to stand during the anthem and has yet to have a player attempt such a protest.

While many N.B.A. players and coaches have been politically vocal, and have spoken in favor of the N.F.L. players, some critics have accused them of hypocrisy considering their league has an even stricter policy. On Tuesday, Curry said the difference is that the N.B.A. has been supportive of political messaging in the past, and that he is confident that support will continue.

"I would assume if somebody wanted to demonstrate or protest during the anthem," Curry said, "that there would be an opportunity to have that discussion and understand what the player wants to express in that moment and that the league would support that player while they're doing it."

N.B.A. Commissioner Adam Silver discussed the matter at a news conference before the finals, pointing out that the rule predated not just his tenure but also the reign of David Stern, as Larry O'Brien had put the standing requirement in the rule book when he was in charge of the league. Silver said he considered the anthem a moment of unity rather than patriotism — he cited the statistic that 25 percent of the league's players were born outside the United States — and said the league did its best to support its players through community actions.

"I'm only an observer in terms of what I see and read about what's happening in the N.F.L.," he said. "But our emphasis at least has been on constructive activities in our communities. There has been no discussion with our Players Association about changing our existing rule."

The N.B.A. did not fine or punish players for wearing "I Can't Breathe" T-shirts over their warm-ups in 2014. The shirts, which technically violated the league's uniform policy, were a reference to the killing of Eric Garner on Staten Island.

Curry believes the important thing with all of these issues, be it anthem demonstrations or White House visits, is for the actual issues to be made clear, and for the truth to win out over political rhetoric. He cited a tweet by Torrey Smith, the former Eagles receiver, that debunked some of the claims made in the White House's statement about the team's disinvitation.

"I think that's important," Curry said. "If you focus on who is saying the right things, you shouldn't get lost in the noise that's going on right now."

Curry's coach, Steve Kerr, believes the visits — of which the Warriors made one after their title in 2015 — can resume once Mr. Trump is out of office.

"I think we all look forward to the day when we can go back to just having a celebration of athletic achievement," he said, adding, "So it will be nice when we can just get back to normal in three years."

Trump Mocks LeBron James's Intelligence and Calls Don Lemon 'Dumbest Man' on TV

BY CHRISTINA CARON | AUG. 4, 2018

PRESIDENT TRUMP LASHED out at the basketball star LeBron James in a scathing attack on Twitter on Friday night after Mr. James criticized the president in an interview on CNN.

In a wide-ranging interview with Don Lemon, an anchor on CNN, Mr. James spoke about a school for at-risk children that he recently helped open in his hometown, Akron, Ohio, in a partnership between his philanthropic foundation and the city's public schools. During the interview on Monday, he also said Mr. Trump was using sports to divide the country.

The interview was aired again on Friday night, and Mr. Trump responded on Twitter shortly after, insulting Mr. James's intelligence and that of Mr. Lemon.

"Lebron James was just interviewed by the dumbest man on television, Don Lemon," Mr. Trump wrote. "He made Lebron look smart, which isn't easy to do. I like Mike!"

The reference to "Mike" appeared to be Mr. Trump's way of taking sides in the debate over who is the greatest basketball player of all time: Mr. James or Michael Jordan.

Through a representative, Mr. Jordan told reporters: "I support L.J. He's doing an amazing job for his community."

Mr. Trump has often heralded his own I.Q. and has questioned the intelligence of others, including Jon Stewart and George W. Bush.

His tweet about Mr. James and Mr. Lemon came days after he declared at a campaign rally that Representative Maxine Waters of California, a Democrat who is black, had a "very low I.Q."

The latest attacks, directed at prominent black people, appeared to widen the racial divide that Mr. James spoke about on CNN.

"I would like to know why he considers these two successful black men 'dumb,' " Torrey Smith, a wide receiver for the Carolina Panthers, said on Twitter. "I know why."

Mr. Trump made his comment a day before a scheduled appearance on Saturday night in Ohio — home of the Cleveland Cavaliers and many LeBron James fans — to campaign for Troy Balderson, a state senator who is running in a special election for the House of Representatives.

Mr. Lemon came to Mr. James's defense on Saturday morning, tweeting: "Who's the real dummy? A man who puts kids in classrooms or one who puts kids in cages?" He added the hashtag #BeBest, a reference to an initiative by the first lady, Melania Trump, that aims to help children.

Stephanie Grisham, Ms. Trump's communications director, said in a statement: "It looks like LeBron James is working to do good things on behalf of our next generation and just as she always has, the first lady encourages everyone to have an open dialogue about issues facing children today."

Ms. Grisham added that Ms. Trump would be open to visiting Mr. James's new school in Akron.

During the CNN interview, Mr. James said conversations about race had "taken over" in part because "our president is kind of trying to divide us." "Kind of?" Mr. Lemon said, followed by a chuckle.

"He is," Mr. James said. "He's dividing us."

Mr. James said his involvement in sports was the first time "I ever was around someone white," adding, "And I got an opportunity to see them and learn about them and they got an opportunity to learn about me, and we became very good friends."

Mr. James has been critical of the president in the past. Last September he called Mr. Trump a "bum" after the president appeared to disinvite the N.B.A. championship-winning Golden State Warriors from a traditional White House visit because one of their stars, Stephen Curry, criticized Mr. Trump.

"U bum @StephenCurry30 already said he ain't going!" Mr. James wrote on Twitter. "So therefore ain't no invite. Going to White House was a great honor until you showed up!"

In June, before Mr. James left the Cavaliers for the Los Angeles Lakers, Mr. Curry and Mr. James united during the N.B.A. finals to say that they would boycott the White House.

"I know whoever wins this series, no one wants an invite," Mr. James said at the time. Afterward, Mr. Trump announced that neither team was invited.

On Monday, the same day as the CNN interview, Mr. James told ESPN that he felt compelled to speak out about the Trump administration.

"For someone to try to divide us by using our platform of sport?" he said. "Sport has given me everything I could ever ask for. I couldn't let that happen."

Mr. Trump's tweet on Saturday was swiftly condemned by many on social media, including Dan Rather, the former CBS News anchor, who said the president's words were racist.

"This is apparently what the President of the United States feels the need to share with the world at what should be long past his bedtime? It's a disgrace. It's racist. And it's the product of petty but dangerous hatreds," Mr. Rather wrote. "I repeat this is the PRESIDENT??!?"

Numerous current and former N.B.A. players also denounced the president's tweet.

A sign of an insecure human being is one who attacks others to make themselves feel better... im just sad that young kids have to see stupid tweets like these and grow up thinking it's okay... forget everything else Donald your setting a bad example for kids our future

— Donovan Mitchell (@spidadmitchell) Aug. 4, 2018

I've been silent about ALL of the DUMB stuff this man has tweeted but THIS is attacking the NBA brotherhood and I'm not rollin'! What an embarrassment...

— Anthony Tolliver (@ATolliver44) Aug. 4, 2018

As of Saturday morning, Mr. James remained silent on the matter.

By late Saturday morning, the president had moved on, and was wishing the Coast Guard a happy birthday on Twitter.

Donald Trump and the Black Athlete

BY MICHAEL POWELL | AUG. 5, 2018

SO WE HAVE MORE EVIDENCE that a master of the dog whistle occupies the White House and that black athletes are a favorite target.

The president, Donald J. Trump, took out after LeBron James on Friday in a way that felt instinctive, as the hound dog pursues the hare. The N.B.A. star had criticized Trump, in measured tones, in an interview with CNN last week. When the anchor Don Lemon asked James what he would say if he were sitting across from Trump, James offered a thin smile.

"I would never sit across from him," he said.

At 11:37 Friday night, after the interview had been rebroadcast, Trump replied with one of those tweets that offer an X-ray of his ego, psyche and soul. "LeBron James was just interviewed by the dumbest man on television, Don Lemon. He made LeBron look smart, which isn't easy to do. I like Mike!"

There was a breathtaking quality to this attack, and not just because white men demeaning the intelligence of black people is one of the oldest and ugliest tropes in American history.

James had appeared on CNN not to criticize this thin-skinned and choleric president but to talk of growing up poor with a single mom and of trying to pay back those who helped him by underwriting a public, noncharter school for at-risk youth in his hometown, Akron, Ohio. His foundation also committed tens of millions of dollars to help provide college scholarships for Akron public school graduates.

James will give every child in this school a bike and a helmet. He is a biking enthusiast for reasons that extend beyond cardiovascular benefit: From James's earliest childhood days, when he lived in a tiny apartment just up an embankment from Cuyahoga Valley railroad tracks, the bike stood as a symbol of freedom. It allowed him to pedal out of his down-at-the-heels neighborhood and explore a larger world.

The bike and sport gave him freedom, he told Lemon, and allowed him to meet and befriend white kids and to see a world laden with possibility. "I got an opportunity to see them and learn about them," he said of white kids, "and they got an opportunity to learn about me, and we became very good friends."

You wonder how Trump could listen to James saying all of this and take away nothing but offense and pique. Then again, it's difficult to know where the line between genuine annoyance and political calculation stands for a man who so willfully stirs the coals of class and racial resentment.

Some of my colleagues in the news media seem at pains to avoid detecting a whiff of race-baiting in Trump's attacks. They cite examples of his attacking the intelligence and demeanor of whites, and his insistent and at times panicky assertions of his own great intelligence.

O.K., sure. We cannot read any man's mind.

It is important as well not to take on the role of yogis, bending so far backward that we pitch into outright credulity. Time and again, this president has questioned black intelligence. And from the former N.F.L. quarterback Colin Kaepernick to the transcendent point guard Stephen Curry, Trump seems to especially enjoy picking public fights with black athletes. Last year he journeyed to Alabama, a place with a historical valise of racial baggage, and offered advice to N.F.L. owners on handling those players who take a knee during the national anthem, players who were largely African-Americans protesting police violence and economic inequality: "Get that son of a bitch off the field right now, he's fired. He's fired!"

He mocked those same owners, most of them white, for going soft on the question of concussions and player brain damage: "Uh-oh, got a little ding on the head?"

In a curious and perhaps subconscious way, that circles back to Trump's attacks on black intelligence. All of this finds a root in American history and culture. The eminent Stanford University historian George M. Fredrickson wrote a groundbreaking book, "The Black Image in the

White Mind," in which he documented the white obsession during the 19th and early 20th centuries with measuring the supposedly deficient size of black brains, the better to undergird "scientific racism."

It has been salutary to watch black athletes and a smaller number of their white comrades show a keen awareness of the larger world, and speak up on matters of politics and culture.

As Trump has attacked black athletes, they have almost as often poked back at him. Last fall, when Curry said he might not attend a ceremony at the White House for the champion Golden State Warriors, Trump ripped Curry and disinvited the team. James, in turn, jumped to the defense of Curry, referring to Trump as "u bum" in a tweet. As athletes find their voice, it's fair enough for politicians to take issue with their views. Trump's default, however, is not to engage but to demean.

It speaks well of his wife, Melania, that she recognized James's CNN interview and his generosity for what it was and praised the player in a statement on Saturday. She spoke of her desire to visit his I Promise school.

As for the president, he attended another political rally in Ohio on Saturday. This time he skipped over James. Maybe he understood that this man is a figure of admiration, even for many white Ohioans, and that another savaging could backfire. Then again, who knows?

Perhaps we should just count ourselves lucky that the president stanched his bile for one hot evening in Ohio.

CHAPTER 5

Personality and Pursuits

LeBron James has let his personality shine through his basketball career. His non-athletic pursuits have shown him to be a charitable person, one clearly connected to his hometown. His commitment to investing in Akron, Ohio, resulted in the opening of his I Promise School. He has also forayed into the world of creative media.

N.B.A. Star, Now Memoirist, on Hometown Court

BY CHARLES MCGRATH | SEPT. 4, 2009

AKRON, OHIO — LeBron James, the most famous alumnus of St. Vincent-St. Mary High School here, goes back to visit all the time. He's such a familiar fixture, dropping by for lunch or to watch basketball practice, that he scarcely attracts attention anymore. Outside, however, he's a traffic hazard. One afternoon last month, a guy cruising by in an S.U.V. caught sight of James, the 6-foot-8 superstar of the Cleveland Cavaliers, outside the school. The driver rolled down the window, yelled "Noooo!" and almost swerved off the road.

St. V., as it's known locally, is a small, private Roman Catholic school on a hill at the edge of the city. The students are mostly white, and mostly come from families prosperous enough to afford the $8,000 tuition, though the school does offer scholarships and financial aid. It's the kind of place that has a golf team as well as a basketball squad, and where there's mandatory religion class and a dress code. No tattoos, no facial hair, no chestnut-size diamond earrings: the grown-up LeBron would have been sent home.

Recalling his first day, in the fall of 1999, James pointed to the cafeteria door. "I came through that door, and thought, 'Wow, there might be a problem.'" He explained: "I had never spent any time with white Americans, and I didn't know anything at all about their culture. I didn't know whether it was the same as ours or different, or what. I didn't think I made a mistake, but it was a big transition."

Most people in Akron had assumed that James would go to John R. Buchtel High School, a largely black public school with a reputation for being a basketball powerhouse. He wound up at St. V. because his friend Dru Joyce III, or Little Dru, as he was called for obvious reasons, worried that he was too short to make the team at Buchtel and persuaded James and two other friends, Sian Cotton and Willie McGee, to attend the Catholic school instead.

In "Shooting Stars" (Penguin Press), a memoir he has written with Buzz Bissinger, which comes out on Tuesday, James now calls that decision an instance of "karma," a providential destiny that he believes has attended him all his life.

"This is the place where all the dreams turned into reality," he said while visiting the school. "If you grow up poor and black in this country, you dream a lot, but you don't really think they're going to come true. This is where it all started — where I began to think I could do it."

"Shooting Stars," which covers much the same ground as "More Than a Game," a documentary film by Kristopher Belman, opening on Oct. 2, says next to nothing about James's N.B.A. career. Like the film, it ends with his last game in high school and is essentially the story of the bond between James and his friends — the Fab Four, as they called themselves, and later, with the addition of Romeo Travis, the Fab Five.

You have to read carefully to realize that James was the star. The team won three state championships and in 2003 USA Today named it the best high school team in the country. In the St. V. locker room, just

James today at St. Vincent-St. Mary High School.

below a graffito that says "King James," is one that reads, "Fab Five 4 Life."

"I didn't want one of those books where it's 'I played this team and I got so many points,' " James said. "That's too typical. People have read those stats before. I wanted the book to be about my childhood, my friends, my feelings."

Mr. Bissinger, the author of "Friday Night Lights," a best-selling book about high school football, was put together with James by his agent. "But the whole story was LeBron's idea," Mr. Bissinger said. "He already had a beginning, a middle, an end. The self-effacing part — that it's about the team, and not just LeBron — that's just his nature. I've met a lot of athletes in my life, and he doesn't have that patina of privilege. He really is a humble guy."

He added: "The book is faithful to the way he thinks, which is what he wanted. But capturing the voice was tricky. I'm sure there are moments when it sounds more like me, even though I was always holding back. I like to write with my own voice — sometimes too much, probably."

Between the ages of 5 and 8, James, the only child of a single mother, moved 12 times. For a while he boarded with another family, the Walkers, whom he now considers part of his fortunate karma. Akron, James writes, wasn't even on the map in some of his school-books, and already some of the Akron he remembers has vanished. His grandmother's house on Hickory Street, where he was born, was condemned and bulldozed. The Elizabeth Park projects, where he lived for a while, were leveled and replaced with condos. What used to be a basketball court at the corner of Silver Street and Doyle is now a weedy vacant lot.

But James still lives in the Tire City and keeps up old connections. His personal assistant is Randy Mims, whom he met when James was 5. Maverick Carter, a high school teammate, handles his business affairs. And Otis Carter, Maverick's father, who used to pick up LeBron in the morning and drive him to school, still drives him around sometimes, only in a much slicker ride: an Audi A8.

As a boy, James says, he used to walk by car lots and fantasize; he said of his current fleet, "You name it, I got one."

With Mr. Carter at the wheel, he made a quick tour of some remaining landmarks on the city's west South Side: the Lincoln-Mercury dealership where he used to look at the new cars, the McDonald's at the corner of Aqueduct and West Market.

"I remember when that place opened," James said. "Those golden arches were like the pearly gates."

Mr. Carter pulled into the parking lot at the Spring Hill Apartments, a severe, Soviet-looking housing block, and James got out and pointed up to the sixth floor.

"Top right — that's where I lived from 6th grade until 12th," he said. "Spring Hill 602. The apartment was about 300 square feet, but the great thing was that from up there, you could see part of the city. This was where the stability started. I knew my mom was going to be there every single day. I had my own key that I wore around my neck. Having your own key to your own crib — that's the greatest thing in the world. And you learn responsibility, because you don't dare lose that key."

He paused a moment and said, shaking his head, "My house now is almost as big as this whole place."

But the places that struck the strongest chord were the hoops shrines: the Summit Lake Community Center, where James played as an 8-year-old; the Ed Davis Community Center, home court of Little Dru's team, then his arch-rivals; the linoleum-floored Salvation Army gym, right around the corner from St. V, though James didn't know it at the time. Still more karma.

"I'm not the same person I was then," James said. "I've moved on to being a man. I have more responsibility. But I believe that everything happens for a reason, and my struggles here in this city helped to make me who I am. My teammates and I got to see the light at the end of the tunnel. We all loved basketball, we all had the same goal, and when you have six or seven guys with that much in common, all staying on the right track, you can accomplish a lot."

LeBron James and His Alter Egos Star in an Internet Animated Series

BY DAVE ITZKOFF | JAN. 17, 2011

WHAT DOES LEBRON JAMES dream about, other than sliding that first National Basketball Association championship ring onto his finger and perhaps riding in luxury automobiles with more generous leg room? How about donning a different kind of uniform and becoming a superhero?

"I think everybody, even grown-ups now, today all wish they could be a superhero," Mr. James, the Miami Heat forward and six-time N.B.A. All-Star, said in a recent telephone interview. "I definitely had that imagination of, like, wow, it would be great to look over a city and take down the bad guys. Absolutely, I had those visions."

In his latest venture, Mr. James won't be fighting crime Batman-style (even if he could probably afford it), but he still hopes to bring inspiration to his young fans. He is taking his talents to the Internet in a new Web-based animated series that will revisit some of his best-known off-the-court performances while featuring socially conscious messages.

The cartoon series, called "The LeBrons" and planned for a spring debut on its own YouTube channel and Mr. James's Web site, lebronjames.com, will revive the characters from a popular series of Nike commercials in which Mr. James played four versions of himself: the youthful and wide-eyed Kid LeBron; the physically adept Athlete LeBron; the smooth and savvy Business LeBron; and an ornery elder statesman called Wise LeBron.

"I'm mostly a kid at heart," Mr. James said of these manifestations, "and I'm the athlete, of course, that everyone sees. But I also have a business side, a cool side, and I love antique stuff and classical music. I guess that's the old man side of me."

"The LeBrons," whose first season will consist of 10 episodes of five to six minutes each, will center on the world of 16-year-old Kid LeBron and his life in Akron, Ohio, using authentic locations from that city, where Mr. James was born and raised.

Like a latter-day "Fat Albert and the Cosby Kids," each episode will convey a message — the value of staying in school, staying off drugs or sticking by your family — while its character design and wry sensibility owe an inspirational debt to "The Boondocks," the satirical comic strip and television series created by Aaron McGruder.

" 'The Boondocks' is very edgy," Mr. James said, "but it has some great points, too, and if you can extract yourself from how edgy it is, you can find that point and you can use it."

Behind the scenes, "The LeBrons" will be produced by Mr. James's production company, Spring Hill Productions, and Believe Entertainment Group. That company's founders, Dan Goodman and Bill Masterson, have helped other entertainment figures translate their online popularity into digital shows, including "Seth MacFarlane's Cavalcade of Cartoon Comedy," a series of online shorts from Mr. MacFarlane, the "Family Guy" creator and star.

"There's a lot of folks out there that have great ideas," Mr. Masterson said, describing how his company finds its creative partners, "but how those ideas can come together with their audience — is there an audience that marketers and advertisers really care about? — play a role in how we decide to move forward."

Mr. James obviously brings a big dose of celebrity to anything he takes part in. But it is his persistent presence on social networks like Twitter and Facebook that has helped cultivate millions of online fans, and that, Mr. Goodman and Mr. Masterson said, will help make "The LeBrons" attractive to the Web-based sponsorships it needs. The series already has sponsors in Hewlett-Packard and Intel, and some proceeds from the show will be used to buy their computers for Boys & Girls Clubs of America.

The other challenge for "The LeBrons" is simply finding the time to work with Mr. James, who will also provide the voice of the Business LeBron character and appear in live-action segments in the series.

"We figure out how to find time," Mr. Goodman said. "We've been on set at Nike shoots, we've been in Miami multiple times, we've been to away games. Wherever we can accommodate the schedule, we make time for him."

On those rare occasions during the N.B.A. season when Mr. James has downtime, he can often be found watching cartoons, whether he is sharing an episode of "SpongeBob Squarepants" or "Ben 10" with his children or treating himself to an animated adventure of Batman, a favorite character.

Asked to name his all-time favorite cartoon, Mr. James cast his vote for "Tom and Jerry," an animated series that embodies his competitive spirit as well as a lead character who shares his winning ways, if not his physical proportions.

"I kind of always rooted for Jerry, man," Mr. James said. "Even though Tom was the underdog, Jerry was much smaller."

LeBron James Developing TV Series for Starz

BY DAVE ITZKOFF | SEPT. 3, 2013

HAVING FULFILLED HIS GOAL of winning an NBA championship a couple of times over, LeBron James is taking his talents to cable television. The Starz cable channel said on Tuesday — not in an hourlong TV special, but in a news release — that it was working with Mr. James, the Miami Heat forward and four-time NBA most valuable player, to develop a half-hour comedy series called "Survivor's Remorse." This series, Starz said, will "explore the complexity, comedy and drama of an experience that everyone reads about, but few understand — what truly happens when you make it out." The network said this scripted series will chronicle two fictional cousins who grew up in a tough Philadelphia neighborhood and, having since achieved fame and fortune, now struggle "with the rewards of money, stardom, love and, occasionally, the guilt of having 'made it.'"

"Survivor's Remorse," which is still in development and has not yet been ordered as a series, will be produced by Mr. James and Maverick Carter, his childhood friend and business manager; as well as Tom Werner, the "Cosby Show" producer turned chairman of the Boston Red Sox; and Mike O'Malley, the comic actor who has appeared on "Glee" and "Justified."

Mr. James said in a statement that "Survivor's Remorse" would offer "a story that needed to be told." Among his favorite shows, he cited "Boardwalk Empire," "24," "Scandal" and "Magic City," a Starz series that ended this summer.

Look Homeward, LeBron

OPINION | BY ROSS DOUTHAT | JULY 12, 2014

ONE OF THE MORE significant migrations in recent American history doesn't involve pioneers heading West, refugees seeking sanctuary, or Joad-like families rambling in search of work. It involves the trajectory of our nation's most talented citizens, who since the 1970s have been clustering ever more densely in certain favored cities, and gradually abandoning the places in between.

In a mid-2000s piece for The Atlantic, Richard Florida, long a booster of "creative class" conurbations, noted that in 1970 college graduates were distributed pretty evenly around the country, but that three decades later they were much more concentrated. A few regions (the BosWash Northeast, the Bay Area, etc.) were destinations of choice for the well educated, and large swaths of the country emphatically were not. In Washington, D.C., and San Francisco, he noted, half the population had college degrees; for Detroit and Cleveland, the figures were 11 percent and 14 percent.

This migration has happened for understandable personal and professional reasons (said the pundit writing from a coffee shop in northeastern Washington, D.C.), and the dense professional networks it has created have arguably been good for certain kinds of economic dynamism.

But elite self-segregation, and what Charles Murray has dubbed the "coming apart" of the professional and working classes, has also contributed to America's growing social problems — hardening lines of class and culture, adding layers of misunderstanding and mistrust to an already polarized polity, and leaching brains and social capital from communities that need them most.

Which brings us to the fascinating story of LeBron James.

The basketball superstar's trajectory up until Friday looked like the entire migration of the talented in miniature (well, a 6-foot-8 miniature). A child of depressed northeastern Ohio, with its struggling cities and declining population, James grew up to be drafted by the Cleveland Cavaliers, played for his home-state team for seven brilliant but championship-free seasons, and then famously bolted for a richer, more glamorous locale.

And why? Not just for the money and amenities, but for the professional network. Like superstars in less-athletic fields, James felt that his productivity would be magnified by the right partnerships — in his case, by sharing a court with fellow stars Chris Bosh and Dwyane Wade. And four N.B.A. finals appearances and two rings later, it's clear he judged correctly.

But now he's making the migration in reverse, returning to the battered Midwestern city he famously betrayed. And strikingly, his statement announcing the move doubled as a kind of communitarian manifesto, implicitly critiquing the values underlying elite self-segregation in America:

> *My presence can make a difference in Miami, but I think it can mean more where I'm from. I want kids in Northeast Ohio ... to realize that there's no better place to grow up. Maybe some of them will come home after college and start a family or open a business ... Our community, which has struggled so much, needs all the talent it can get.*
>
> *In Northeast Ohio, nothing is given. Everything is earned. You work for what you have.*
>
> *I'm ready to accept the challenge. I'm coming home.*

Now I don't want to make too much of an exhortation that is, of course, partially just a rich athlete's brand-managing P.R. Especially since homecomings are fraught, complicated undertakings — for superstars even more than ordinary mortals, perhaps — and this one is as likely to end with LeBron feuding with ownership or forcing a trade as with a championship.

Moreover, even if everything goes smoothly on the court, LeBron's "hard work" will be rather more richly rewarded than the typical Ohioan's, and he'll be "coming home" while still living, really, in the secure and gilded bubble of the rich and famous. So for a future college graduate deciding between staying on the Acela Corridor or coming back to Akron or Youngstown to raise a family, LeBron's example is symbolically inspiring without being terribly relevant to the hazards of real life.

But with all those caveats, there will be a spillover effect of some sort from his decision. Even if it only happens on the margins, LeBron really did just make a down-at-the-heels part of America a slightly better place to live and work and settle.

And the return of the King is also a reminder that social trends, like careers, aren't arrows that fly in one direction only. As real estate prices rise insanely on the coasts, as telecommuting becomes more plausible for more people, as once-storied cities hit bottom and rebound ... well, there could be more incentives for less-extraordinary professionals to imitate this heartland native's unexpected return.

At the very least there's nothing written that says we have to come apart forever. Or that some Americans with less extraordinary but still substantial gifts can't find a way, like LeBron, to take those talents home again.

ROSS DOUTHAT is an Op-Ed columnist for The New York Times.

In Going Home, James May Be Ending an Exile From Himself

BY WILLIAM C. RHODEN | JULY 12, 2014

FORGIVENESS IS NOT ONE of my strong suits, so the idea that LeBron James would go back to Cleveland was unfathomable, even with Miami's limitations.

On the other hand, post-Donald Sterling, I have become an enthusiastic advocate of players wringing every nickel out of ownership. No givebacks, no pay cuts. In that respect, I was pleased to see Carmelo Anthony make Phil Jackson and the Knicks sweat before agreeing to return for a fat contract.

But while Anthony's decision was no doubt determined largely by dollars, James's decision to return to Cleveland is an intriguing, emotional gambit. James is either coldly pragmatic or more of an altruist than I could have imagined.

The images from 2010 are still emblazoned in my mind: Cleveland fans burning James's replica jersey just because he was leaving for a better opportunity in Miami. Nationally televised images of James's likeness being torn down and dumped in garbage cans.

The so-called leader of the franchise, Dan Gilbert, the Cavaliers' owner, fanned the flames and played to the crowd by writing a scathing letter publicly disparaging James as "our former hero" and describing his move as a "cowardly betrayal."

James, in his statement on Sports Illustrated's website, implied that forgiveness and understanding formed the basis of his decision to return to Ohio.

"It was easy to say, 'O.K., I don't want to deal with these people ever again,' " he said. "But then you think about the other side. What if I were a kid who looked up to an athlete, and that athlete made me want to do better in my own life, and then he left? How would I react?"

James said he and Gilbert met "face-to-face, man-to-man."

"We've talked it out," James said. "Everybody makes mistakes. I've made mistakes as well. Who am I to hold a grudge?"

On Friday, I reached out to William Cutter, a professor of literature and human relations at Hebrew Union College in Los Angeles. How heavily did he think forgiveness figured into James's decision? We met about three years ago and often debate the theological and philosophical underpinnings of sports. In the case of Gilbert and James, Cutter said that forgiveness was a two-way street.

"A piece of forgiveness in the classic Jewish tradition is forgiving the person, and the person joining the act by an act of repentance," he said. "Not only repentance, but pledging not to do it again."

Was giving James a big contract Gilbert's version of repentance?

"I'm wondering if this isn't just what James Burns of Williams College once called transactional," Cutter said. "Is there anything spiritual in this, or is it purely transactional?"

Cutter did allow for the complexity of James's situation.

"I think often people have mixed motives," he said. "Yes, there's more money; yes, he is from Cleveland; and yes, he may have felt in exile. You can be in exile even if geographically you're not in exile."

Of all the rationales for James's homecoming, a sense of feeling exiled seems plausible. As much as I was convinced that James would stay in Miami — for the milder climate, for what appeared to be a more upscale, high-profile lifestyle — there never was a sense that he was of Miami.

"You can be in exile from yourself," Cutter said.

In this case LeBron could say, "I felt in exile."

The Rev. Calvin O. Butts III, the pastor of the Abyssinian Baptist Church in New York, compared James's departure and return to the New Testament story of the prodigal son.

"He set out to achieve something, made a radical break at home," Butts said of James. "People were angry and hurt. He won his rings, but maybe there was something missing in his life. He didn't find it in Miami, not in L.A., not in New York. He said, 'I have to go back home,' and they welcome him with open arms."

One of the most surprising responses to James's return to Cleveland came from my longtime friend Mike Brown, who has deep roots in coaching. Brown was an assistant coach at Seton Hall under P. J. Carlesimo; an assistant at Vermont, Cincinnati, San Francisco, Kansas and Mississippi State; head coach at Central Connecticut State and Hunter College; and associate coach at Fordham. By no stretch of the imagination could he be called romantic or sentimental when it comes to the business of basketball.

Yet Brown said he was moved by James's letter, especially the part when James said: "I feel my calling here goes above basketball. My presence can make a difference in Miami, but I think it can mean more where I'm from. I want kids in Northeast Ohio, like the hundreds of Akron third-graders I sponsor through my foundation, to realize that there's no better place to grow up. Maybe some of them will come home after college and start a family or open a business. That would make me smile. Our community, which has struggled so much, needs all the talent it can get."

Brown said James's statement "brought tears to my eyes."

"I was overwhelmed," he said. "I thought to myself: 'Finally a black athlete who gets it. Finally a black athlete who is taking responsibility for being someone who can and does make a difference in the lives of his people.' "

Brown acknowledged that James may simply have expressed those sentiments "to make it easier to leave Miami."

"But if just a shred of what he said was honest and from the heart," Brown added, "he now joins Jackie Robinson, Arthur Ashe, Jim Brown, Muhammad Ali, Bill Russell and Oscar Robertson in a class of black athletes who understood their responsibility to their people and their communities."

Time will tell.

Time will tell whether James was sincere, whether Gilbert is repentant and whether Cleveland fans appreciate the significance of James's return, above and beyond the championship he may or may not bring.

"For today," Brown said, "he elevated himself to the pantheon of athletes who understand that it's not just about how many shoes you sell or endorsements you have. It's about how many people you help, how many lives you change, and the hope you give people."

And while Anthony didn't give Knicks fans hope, just assurances that the ship won't be sinking, there is plenty of hope and good will in Cleveland at the moment.

It's summertime. There's dancing in the street. Many of the dancers are the same ones who burned James's jersey and cheered Gilbert's letter. They will be the ones throwing darts at James if Cleveland isn't in the N.B.A. finals in two or three seasons.

For the time being, though, spirits are high and optimism is soaring, almost as if the events of 2010 had never happened.

The Cavaliers will spend a small fortune to bring back their prodigal son. Cleveland is eager to make him a hero.

This may be an instance where it's best for everyone to forgive and, more important, to forget.

Will the LeBron James Stimulus Be Good for Cleveland?

BY BINYAMIN APPELBAUM | NOV. 4, 2014

WHEN LEBRON JAMES announced his return to the Cleveland Cavaliers in July, fans celebrated by hanging banners, getting drunk and digging old jerseys out of purgatory. They ran into the streets, honked horns and hugged strangers. And some of them started trying to figure out just how much money was about to rain down on Cleveland. According to one estimate, the return of the "king," as James is known, will add $500 million a year to the city's economy. "When people say this is just about an athlete making money, there's more to it than that," said Edward FitzGerald, the Cuyahoga County executive, at a news conference devoted to the anticipated windfall. "Other people will make a living."

James is certainly a good investment for the Cavaliers, who will probably cover his $20.6 million salary just from increased ticket sales. The last season James played in Cleveland, after all, the Cavs sold every available regular-season seat at an average price of $55.95, earning about $47 million. Last season, the Cavaliers sold just 84 percent at an average price of just $43.31, for a decline of $16 million. This year, season tickets sold out the day James announced his return, and demand is so overwhelming that the team is raffling the remaining single-game tickets so that everyone in Cleveland has a fair chance. Everything else is gravy: playoff games, sponsorships, jersey sales and the team's local broadcast rights, serendipitously scheduled for renegotiation at the end of next season.

What FitzGerald and some other Cleveland boosters envision, though, is a LeBron stimulus that enriches the city as a whole. Start, for example, with the restaurants along East Fourth Street, near the arena, whose business dropped significantly after James bolted for Miami. Scalpers are happy, too, and owners of nearby stores that

A chalk wall at Klutch Sports Group's office featuring quotes from James's essay in which he announced he was returning to Cleveland.

sell T-shirts and jewelry also expect sales to pick up. To get that $500 million estimate, LeRoy Brooks, an emeritus professor of finance at John Carroll University, just outside Cleveland, assumed that all these people making more money will spend it in Cleveland, multiplying the James effect. Brooks told me he now thinks James will add between $163 million and $426 million to the regional economy. He said that he made the first estimate in haste, "on the day after my first grandson was born." FitzGerald's staff estimated a more modest bounce. The LeBron stimulus, they concluded, could reach $285 million, including the creation of about 550 new jobs.

Certain individuals have changed a city's fortunes. John D. Rockefeller helped to drive Cleveland's rise as an industrial power. Bill Gates sparked Seattle's high-tech transformation. Dan Gilbert, the founder of Quicken Loans and owner of the Cavs, has purchased a large chunk of downtown Detroit, which he is slowly renovating and repopulating.

But James is not an entrepreneur: He's a wage-earning entertainer who manufactures jump shots and no-look passes. And there is a limit to how much difference one more union member can make. Last year, the Cleveland area's economic output was about $123 billion. By the most generous estimates, the return of James would expand output by less than one half of 1 percent. The biggest economic engine in postindustrial Cleveland is probably the Cleveland Clinic, a sprawling treatment and research center that estimates its own annual impact at about $10.5 billion, or 8 percent of the regional total. So the best case is that the return of James has about the same effect as a modest hospital expansion.

Moreover, other experts regard these estimates as wildly inflated. Victor Matheson, an economist at the College of the Holy Cross in Massachusetts, calls it "the worst economic-impact estimate ever," because most of the projected spending is just dollars sloshing around northeast Ohio. What's good for downtown Cleveland, in other words, is bad for the suburbs. "It's just going to result in a redistribution of entertainment spending from other activities to the Cavs," said Edward W. Hill, dean of the Levin College of Urban Affairs at Cleveland State University. "My wife is now beating me on top of the head to make sure that I get our tickets, which will mean one less dinner together at a restaurant as we go to the Cavs instead." It's also worth noting that Cleveland is paying for the right to host James. Cuyahoga County borrowed $120 million in the early 1990s to build the team's arena, and it still owes more than half that sum. Earlier this year, voters approved extending a tax that is projected to raise $260 million for the city's three stadiums. Any benefits of James's return are, in effect, a return on that investment.

But Hill does see a more intangible benefit. Nike paid James roughly $13 million a year to endorse its products during his first stint in Cleveland. He has since signed a new deal that is said to be even more lucrative. Now James is effectively endorsing Cleveland too. People looking for basketball shoes may be more likely to value his endorsement than people looking for a place to live or to locate their businesses, but every little bit helps. "We've had the best public relations for Cleveland since World War II," FitzGerald told a local radio station a few days after James announced his return. On a recent trip to Guangzhou, China, Hill said he saw a man in a park, dressed in a James jersey with "Cleveland" emblazoned across the front. "For a midsize metropolitan area, the fact that you are affiliated with a global brand gives you name recognition that cuts across the clutter," he said.

The return of James, which was announced just a week after the news that the 2016 Republican National Convention will take place in Cleveland, could also change the way residents think about their city. And economically speaking, mood matters. John Maynard Keynes regarded "animal spirits" as a primary motor of growth. When people are feeling good, they are more likely to take risks and make investments. Officials hope the excitement will stoke continued residential development in the gaptoothed downtown, where the population has roughly doubled since 2000. "I want kids in Northeast Ohio ... to realize that there's no better place to grow up," James wrote when announcing his decision in Sports Illustrated. "Maybe some of them will come home after college and start a family or open a business."

Cleveland, in some sense, is hoping to follow the paradigm of Manchester, England, another downtrodden factory town that is now best known for its soccer teams. Manchester United sells 30 percent of its tickets to people from outside the region and, seeking to capitalize on the tourism, the city opened a national soccer museum in 2012. The region's economic-development brochures often feature an image of Old Trafford, United's stadium, and economic-development officials sometimes follow the team on road trips. This kind of glamour by association is an easy way to start a conversation, although a recent economic study of the city cautioned that it can only take that conversation so far. "Whenever it comes down to the actual completion of a deal, it is the competitiveness of the offering that matters," it said.

But there's an important difference between hosting the world's most famous soccer team and the world's most famous basketball player. Franchises stick around, but kings do not rule forever. Cleveland has just a few years to capitalize.

BINYAMIN APPELBAUM is an economics reporter for The Times.

The N.B.A.'s Decider: How LeBron James Controls Fortunes

BY SCOTT CACCIOLA | JUNE 29, 2018

LEBRON JAMES REPORTEDLY informed the Cleveland Cavaliers, his current employer, on Friday that he was exercising his option to become a free agent rather than remaining under his current contract for another year.

The decision vigorously revived an annual phenomenon in the N.B.A. that is unknown to every other sports league: One person grabs hold of the collective psyche of fans, team officials and even civic leaders, single-handedly in control of their fortunes.

If James decides to join your team, you are instantly an N.B.A. title contender, and your city feels the lift. If James decides to leave your team, you are the Jackson 5 after Michael left the band, or "The West Wing" after Aaron Sorkin's departure — looked up to fondly with nostalgia but otherwise obsolete.

James, 33, has successfully turned the high-stakes drama of free agency into his own reality show. He is the N.B.A.'s best player and its most captivating presence. He is also one of its savviest power brokers, and he has developed a summer ritual of holding the rest of the N.B.A. and entire metropolitan areas in a state of expectancy as he weighs his options every July.

"This one guy not only controls the league, but part of our economy, too," said Jason Herron, 45, a longtime Cavaliers season ticket-holder and the general manager of a car dealership.

Herron said he recently talked to a bar owner in downtown Cleveland who told Herron that he might have to lay off part of his staff next winter if James leaves town.

"It's been a heck of a ride," Herron said. "We just don't want it to end."

James chose to enter free agency — which officially begins Sunday at 12:01 a.m. Eastern — rather than exercise his $35.6 million option to stay under his current contract for another year. He can re-sign with the Cavaliers, but he also has a host of suitors, headlined by the Los Angeles Lakers.

Basketball is different from other team sports. The Los Angeles Angels can have Mike Trout, the best player in baseball, and still be thoroughly mediocre because he gets only four or five at-bats a game. An N.F.L. team can sign a star quarterback and still fall short of making the playoffs because he cannot throw the ball to himself, and he won't be on the field to play defense.

But when free-agent maneuvers involve the very top tier of N.B.A. players, those players' decisions can have an outsize impact on individual teams, the league more broadly and even entire cities.

Kevin Durant is one of the more famous examples. Since he jumped to Golden State in 2016, the Warriors have won two straight championships. Without him, the Oklahoma City Thunder, the team he departed, have not won a playoff series.

Players like James, Durant and precious few others forge title contenders — which means higher ticket and merchandise sales, higher TV ratings, more tourists coming to see the show, more international media exposure for the city.

It is technically the off-season for the N.B.A., which means that all the players have dispersed for the summer. No practices, and no games. But the superstar sweepstakes of free agency create a strange rhythm for the league, which finds out in the summer which teams are going to be world-beaters next season — and which ones will be sent spiraling into competitive oblivion for the foreseeable future.

When that superstar sweepstakes involves James, a four-time most valuable player who is capable of dominating games — and who has continually kept the pressure on the Cavaliers to upgrade their roster in recent seasons by signing a series of short contracts — the effect is multiplied many times over.

A team with James is an instant title contender. A team without James — well, you better have a collection of All-Stars already on the roster.

Cleveland is uniquely familiar with both sides of this equation. James, who grew up just outside the city in Akron, spent the first seven seasons of his career with the Cavaliers and led them deep into the playoffs his final five seasons. But in a made-for-TV spectacle known as "The Decision," James announced that he was joining the Miami Heat in 2010. This was the first Summer of LeBron — the first time he was capable of holding sway over the league as a free agent, and it quickly became clear just how much power he wielded.

With James, the Heat went on to win two championships. Without him, the Cavaliers were left in ruins, a perennial resident of the draft lottery as one of the worst teams in the league.

The Cavaliers' fortunes dramatically reversed course when James returned in 2014. Four straight trips to the finals followed, including the franchise's first and only championship in 2016. For three of those seasons, James teamed with Kyrie Irving, a perennial All-Star, to form one of the league's most fearsome duos.

But the dynamics changed last summer when Irving asked for a trade — in part so he could escape James's shadow. The Cavaliers sent Irving to the Boston Celtics.

In his absence, the Cavaliers labored last season to find their footing, even as James played some of his finest basketball. He averaged 27.5 points, 8.6 rebounds and 9.1 assists a game while shooting 54.2 percent from the field. He also played in all 82 regular-season games for the first time in his career.

But the Cavaliers had to shuffle new personnel in and out of the lineup — experiments that often fell flat. The result was a hodgepodge season that James assessed as one of the most challenging of his career. There were many moments when he did not appear to be enjoying himself. And still — *still!* — James managed to haul the Cavaliers into the finals, which might have been one of his most miraculous feats to date.

The only problem was that they got swept by the Warriors, and James appeared to be mulling free agency before the series even ended.

"Every G.M. and every president and every coaching staff is trying to figure out how they can make up the right matchups to compete for a championship," he said at the time.

He might as well have included himself. Nobody in the league is capable of exerting greater influence on teams — and the moves they make, either directly or indirectly — than James, who recently decamped with his family to Anguilla, a British territory in the Caribbean. For all the agita swirling around him, James has seemed very chill. On Thursday night, he shared a video clip of himself on his Instagram account, which has nearly 40 million followers: He was jumping off a cliff, presumably into a warm body of water below.

For the breathless masses who are curious about James's future — and those masses include friends and rivals, coaches and executives, fans and haters — the clip has been parsed with forensic detail: What does it mean? Was he offering some sort of coded message? A metaphor about taking the plunge with a new team?

Or maybe he just wanted to go for a swim. The real news will come soon enough, and James, as usual, will be the one making it.

Ryan Coogler and LeBron James Bringing Back 'Space Jam'

BY SOPAN DEB | SEPT. 19, 2018

EVERYBODY GET UP, it's time to slam again. We've got a real jam going down. Welcome to another "Space Jam."

The long-rumored follow-up to the 1996 classic featuring Michael Jordan and Looney Tunes stars is officially in the works, according to an announcement Wednesday by Springhill Entertainment, LeBron James's production company.

It is unclear what Mr. James's role will be in the movie, although it's a safe bet that he will star and that several other N.B.A. players will make cameos. Terence Nance (HBO's "Random Acts of Flyness") is directing and Ryan Coogler, the director of the massively successful "Black Panther," will be a producer.

"The 'Space Jam' collaboration is so much more than just me and the Looney Tunes getting together and doing this movie," Mr. James said in an interview with The Hollywood Reporter. "It's so much bigger. I'd just love for kids to understand how empowered they can feel and how empowered they can be if they don't just give up on their dreams. And I think Ryan did that for a lot of people."

Mr. James's other recent forays into the entertainment world include "The Shop," an HBO show in which he held court in barbershops to discuss issues of the day. He was also an executive producer of the program. His name appears on several other coming projects, including the HBO Sports documentary "Student Athlete," to be broadcast next month, and a 10-episode competition series, "Million Dollar Mile," which will air on CBS. There is also "Shut Up and Dribble," a three-part Showtime documentary on the role of athlete activism.

Many other N.B.A. players have made the jump to content creation. Andre Iguodala announced a partnership with the Cheddar network last year. Kyrie Irving starred in "Uncle Drew," based on a series of

Pepsi commercials that he helped create. Kobe Bryant, now retired, won an Oscar last year for best animated short with "Dear Basketball."

The "Space Jam" sequel has been rumored for years. Justin Lin, best known for his work on the "The Fast and the Furious" franchise was said to be directing the film in 2016. That same year, Blake Griffin and Jimmy Butler starred in a Foot Locker and Air Jordan commercial featuring Bugs Bunny and referring to the Monstars, the villains in the original film. The Wrap reported rumors of Mr. Nance's involvement last month.

According to The Hollywood Reporter, filming will begin next summer after the N.B.A. season. That makes sense, given that Mr. James also has his day job: trying to bring his new team, the Los Angeles Lakers, a championship.

Glossary

ABCD Camp An elite high school basketball camp that ran from 1984 to 2007 and helped launch many careers.

all-star A term used to denote an excellent player.

assist In basketball, a pass of the ball to a teammate who then scores a basket.

defender In basketball, a team member who plays defense. They steal the ball, deflect passes and block shots.

draft The N.B.A. draft, established in 1947, occurs every year in June. The National Basketball Association picks new players to join teams.

Eastern Conference The Eastern Conference and the Western Conference make up the N.B.A. The Eastern Conference is comprised of fifteen teams split into three divisions: Atlantic, Central and Southeast. Each division has five teams. Each team plays a total of 82 games in a season, with one champion from each conference going to the N.B.A. finals.

fake In basketball, a move used to knock defenders off balance. The player with the ball will fake a jump shot but hold on to the ball.

finals The N.B.A. finals determines the N.B.A. champions. The champions from the Eastern and Western conferences play a best of seven tournament until there is one winner.

free agent A player whose contract has expired under his current team or who terminated his contract in accordance with N.B.A. procedures and is eligible to sign a contract with any team.

game ball The basketball used in a game.

M.V.P. The Most Valuable Player (M.V.P.) Award, given by the N.B.A to the best performing player of the season.

N.B.A. The National Basketball Association (N.B.A.) is a professional basketball association comprised of 30 teams.

playoffs A tournament that determines which teams proceed to the N.B.A. finals. Teams play a best-of-seven elimination tournament, which consists of conference quarterfinals, conference semifinals and conference finals.

point guard One of five player positions in a basketball game. The point guard is responsible for leading the team's offense by passing the ball to teammates in scoring positions.

regular season There are 82 games in the N.B.A.'s regular season. These games determine which teams proceed to the playoffs.

rookie A new player in the N.B.A. who has never played an N.B.A. game before.

Western Conference The Western Conference is comprised of fifteen teams split into three divisions: Northwest, Pacific, and Southwest. Each division has five teams. Each team plays a total of 82 games in a season, with one champion from each conference going to the N.B.A. finals.

Media Literacy Terms

"Media literacy" refers to the ability to access, understand, critically assess and create media. The following terms are important components of media literacy, and they will help you critically engage with the articles in this title.

angle The aspect of a news story that a journalist focuses on and develops.

attribution The method by which a source is identified or by which facts and information are assigned to the person who provided them.

balance Principle of journalism that both perspectives of an argument should be presented in a fair way.

bias A disposition of prejudice in favor of a certain idea, person or perspective.

byline Name of the writer, usually placed between the headline and the story.

caption Identifying copy for a picture; also called a legend or cutline.

chronological order Method of writing a story presenting the details of the story in the order in which they occurred.

column A type of story that is a regular feature, often on a recurring topic, written by the same journalist, generally known as a columnist.

commentary A type of story that is an expression of opinion on recent events by a journalist generally known as a commentator.

credibility The quality of being trustworthy and believable, said of a journalistic source.

critical review A type of story that describes an event or work of art, such as a theater performance, film, concert, book, restaurant, radio or television program, exhibition or musical piece, and offers critical assessment of its quality and reception.

editorial Article of opinion or interpretation.

fake news A fictional or made-up story presented in the style of a legitimate news story, intended to deceive readers; also commonly used to criticize legitimate news because of its perspective or unfavorable coverage of a subject.

feature story Article designed to entertain as well as to inform.

headline Type, usually 18 point or larger, used to introduce a story.

human interest story A type of story that focuses on individuals and how events or issues affect their lives, generally offering a sense of relatability to the reader.

impartiality Principle of journalism that a story should not reflect a journalist's bias and should contain balance.

intention The motive or reason behind something, such as the publication of a news story.

interview story A type of story in which the facts are gathered primarily by interviewing another person or persons.

inverted pyramid A method of writing a story using facts in order of importance, beginning with a lead and then gradually adding paragraphs in order of relevance from most interesting to least interesting.

motive The reason behind something, such as the publication of a news story or a source's perspective on an issue.

news story An article or style of expository writing that reports news, generally in a straightforward fashion and without editorial comment.

op-ed An opinion piece that reflects a prominent individual's opinion on a topic of interest.

paraphrase The summary of an individual's words, with attribution, rather than a direct quotation of their exact words.

plagiarism An attempt to pass another person's work as one's own without attribution.

quotation The use of an individual's exact words indicated by the use of quotation marks and proper attribution.

reliability The quality of being dependable and accurate, said of a journalistic source.

rhetorical device Technique in writing intending to persuade the reader or communicate a message from a certain perspective.

source The origin of the information reported in journalism.

sports reporting A type of story that reports on sporting events or topics related to sports.

style A distinctive use of language in writing or speech; also a news or publishing organization's rules for consistent use of language with regard to spelling, punctuation, typography and capitalization, usually regimented by a house style guide.

tone A manner of expression in writing or speech.

Media Literacy Questions

1. Identify each of the sources in "Remembering King James, Before and After His Crowning" (on page 46) as a primary source or a secondary source. Evaluate the reliability and credibility of each source. How does your evaluation of each source change your perspective on this article?

2. Compare the headlines of "LeBron James to the Lakers: There's Much to Unpack Here" (on page 95) and "One Thing LeBron James Can't Win: A Comparison With Michael Jordan" (on page 132). Which is a more compelling headline, and why? How could the less compelling headline be changed to better draw the reader's interest?

3. "LeBron James Puts on a Lakers Uniform, and a Stoic Mask" (on page 98) features photographs. What do these photographs add to the article?

4. The article "LeBron James and the Superstar Fallacy" (on page 138) is an example of an op-ed. Identify how Will Leitch's attitude and tone help convey his opinion on the topic.

5. Does Michael Powell demonstrate the journalistic principle of impartiality in his article "Donald Trump and the Black Athlete" (on page 179)? If so, how did he do so? If not, what could he have included to make his article more impartial?

6. Does " 'To Me, It Was Racist': N.B.A. Players Respond to Laura Ingraham's Comments on LeBron James" (on page 168) use multiple sources? What are the strengths of using multiple sources in a journalistic piece? What are the weaknesses of relying heavily on only one or a few sources?

7. Often, as a news story develops, a journalist's attitude toward the subject may change. Compare "The Decision Is Reversed, and Cleveland Is in a Forgiving Mood" (on page 59) and "LeBron James Is the Change Fans Want to See in the Basketball World" (on page 107), both by Scott Cacciola. Did new information discovered between the publication of these two articles change Cacciola's perspective?

8. Analyze the authors' reporting in "Cleveland's Venom Validates James's Exit" (on page 50) and "LeBron James Delivered. Now Does He Exit?" (on page 80). Do you think one journalist is more balanced in his reporting than the other? If so, why do you think so?

9. What type of story is "Look Homeward, LeBron" (on page 191)? Can you identify another article in this collection that is the same type of story? What elements helped you come to your conclusion?

10. What is the intention of the article "There Are Lakers Not Named LeBron James — and They Are Not So Bad" (on page 148)? How effectively does it achieve its intended purpose?

11. Does "LeBron James and Stephen Curry Unite Against White House Visits" (on page 171) use multiple sources? What are the strengths of using multiple sources in a journalistic piece? What are the weaknesses of relying heavily on only one or a few sources?

12. What type of story is "LeBron James Is a Sack of Melons" (on page 53)? Can you identify another article in this collection that is the same type of story? What elements helped you come to your conclusion?

Citations

All citations in this list are formatted according to the Modern Language Association's (MLA) style guide.

BOOK CITATION

THE NEW YORK TIMES EDITORIAL STAFF. *LeBron James.* New York: New York Times Educational Publishing, 2020.

ONLINE ARTICLE CITATIONS

ALCINDOR, YAMICHE. "LeBron James, Calling for Hope and Unity, Endorses Hillary Clinton." *The New York Times*, 2 Oct. 2016, www.nytimes.com/2016/10/03/us/politics/lebron-hillary-clinton.html.

ANDERSON, SAM. "LeBron James Is a Sack of Melons." *The New York Times*, 5 July 2012, www.nytimes.com/2012/07/08/magazine/lebron-james-is-a-sack-of-melons.html.

APPELBAUM, BINYAMIN. "Will the LeBron James Stimulus Be Good for Cleveland?" *The New York Times*, 4 Nov. 2014, www.nytimes.com/2014/11/09/magazine/will-the-lebron-james-stimulus-be-good-for-cleveland.html.

ARATON, HARVEY. "In Year 1, James Pumped the Volume to 11." *The New York Times*, 15 Apr. 2004, https://www.nytimes.com/2004/04/15/sports/sports-of-the-times-in-year-1-james-pumped-the-volume-to-11.html.

ARATON, HARVEY. "LeBron James Is So Luminous, Yet So Trapped by the Public's Glare." *The New York Times*, 21 Jan. 2016, www.nytimes.com/2016/01/22/sports/basketball/lebron-jamess-moves-keep-cavaliers-under-the-microscope.html.

ARATON, HARVEY. "One Thing LeBron James Can't Win: A Comparison With Michael Jordan." *The New York Times*, 28 May 2017, www.nytimes.com/2017/05/28/sports/basketball/lebron-james-michael-jordan-comparison.html.

ARATON, HARVEY. "Remembering King James, Before and After His Crowning." *The New York Times*, 16 June 2015, www.nytimes.com/2015/06/17

/sports/basketball/remembering-king-james-before-and-after-his
-crowning.html.

ARATON, HARVEY. "Skipping Straight to the James Era, With One Caveat."
The New York Times, 20 Feb. 2005, www.nytimes.com/2005/02/20
/sports/basketball/skipping-straight-to-the-james-era-with-one
-caveat.html.

BECK, HOWARD. "Cavaliers Sinking, Despite James's Efforts." *The New York
Times*, 15 Apr. 2005, www.nytimes.com/2005/04/15/sports/basketball
/cavaliers-sinking-despite-jamess-efforts.html.

BRANDON, LILLY. "It's Decisions, Decisions for LeBron James." *The New
York Times*, 12 July 2002, www.nytimes.com/2002/07/12/sports
/basketball-it-s-decisions-decisions-for-lebron-james.html.

BROMWICH, JONAH ENGEL. " 'To Me, It Was Racist': N.B.A. Players Respond
to Laura Ingraham's Comments on LeBron James." *The New York Times*,
16 Feb. 2018, www.nytimes.com/2018/02/16/sports/basketball/lebron
-laura-ingraham.html.

BROUSSARD, CHRIS. "James Answers Hype With Standout Debut." *The New
York Times*, 30 Oct. 2003, www.nytimes.com/2003/10/30/sports/basketball
-james-answers-hype-with-standout-debut.html.

BROUSSARD, CHRIS. "James's Debut Leaves Critics Gushing." *The New York
Times*, 31 Oct. 2003, www.nytimes.com/2003/10/31/sports/pro-basketball
-james-s-debut-leaves-critics-gushing.html.

CACCIOLA, SCOTT. "Cavaliers Defeat Warriors to Win Their First N.B.A. Title."
The New York Times, 19 June 2016, www.nytimes.com/2016/06/20/sports
/basketball/golden-state-warriors-cleveland-cavaliers-nba-championship
.html.

CACCIOLA, SCOTT. "The Decision Is Reversed, and Cleveland Is in a Forgiving
Mood." *The New York Times*, 11 July 2014, www.nytimes.com/2014/07/12
/sports/basketball/lebron-james-to-return-to-cleveland-cavaliers-leaving
-miami-heat.html.

CACCIOLA, SCOTT. "LeBron James Awards Game Balls to Friends and Foes."
The New York Times, 10 June 2016, https://www.nytimes.com/2016/06/11
/sports/basketball/lebron-james-cleveland-cavaliers-nba-finals.html.

CACCIOLA, SCOTT. "LeBron James Boycotts Donald Trump's Hotel, Then Beats
Up Knicks." *The New York Times*, 7 Dec. 2016, www.nytimes.com/2016
/12/07/sports/basketball/lebron-james-trump-hotel-phil-jackson.html.

CACCIOLA, SCOTT. "LeBron James Has Plenty of Patience. For Now." *The New*

York Times, 19 Oct. 2018, www.nytimes.com/2018/10/19/sports/la-lakers
-lebron-james.html.

CACCIOLA, SCOTT. "LeBron James Is a One-Man Show. Sometimes That Is
the Problem." *The New York Times*, 24 Apr. 2018, https://www.nytimes
.com/2018/04/24/sports/lebron-james-cavaliers.html.

CACCIOLA, SCOTT. "LeBron James Is Hurt in Lakers' Blowout of the Warriors."
The New York Times, 25 Dec. 2018, www.nytimes.com/2018/12/25/sports
/lebron-james-injury-lakers.html.

CACCIOLA, SCOTT. "LeBron James Is the Change Fans Want to See in the
Basketball World." *The New York Times*, 22 Nov. 2018, www.nytimes.com
/2018/11/22/sports/basketball/lebron-james-cleveland-lakers.html.

CACCIOLA, SCOTT. "The N.B.A.'s Decider: How LeBron James Controls Fortunes." *The New York Times*, 29 June 2018, www.nytimes.com/2018/06/29
/sports/lebron-james-decision.html.

CACCIOLA, SCOTT. "There Are Lakers Not Named LeBron James — and They
Are Not So Bad." *The New York Times*, 26 Dec. 2018, www.nytimes.com
/2018/12/26/sports/lakers-lebron-james-.html.

CACCIOLA, SCOTT. "Why Kobe Bryant Fans Don't Like LeBron James."
The New York Times, 13 July 2018, www.nytimes.com/2018/07/13/sports
/lakers-lebron-james-kobe-bryant.html.

CACCIOLA, SCOTT, AND JONAH ENGEL BROMWICH. "LeBron James Responds to
Racial Vandalism: 'Being Black in America Is Tough.' " *The New York Times*,
31 May 2017, www.nytimes.com/2017/05/31/sports/lebron-racist
-graffiti-home.html.

CARON, CHRISTINA. "Trump Mocks LeBron James's Intelligence and Calls
Don Lemon 'Dumbest Man' on TV." *The New York Times*, 4 Aug. 2018,
www.nytimes.com/2018/08/04/sports/donald-trump-lebron-james
-twitter.html.

CLAREY, CHRISTOPHER. "LeBron James Delivered on His Promise in 2016."
The New York Times, 22 Dec. 2016, www.nytimes.com/2016/12/22/sports
/lebron-james-2016-nba-finals.html.

DEB, SOPAN. "Ryan Coogler and LeBron James Bringing Back 'Space Jam.' "
The New York Times, 19 Sept. 2018, www.nytimes.com/2018/09/19
/movies/ryan-coogler-and-lebron-james-a-new-space-jam.html.

DOUTHAT, ROSS. "Look Homeward, LeBron." *The New York Times*, 12 July
2014, www.nytimes.com/2014/07/13/opinion/sunday/ross-douthat-look
-homeward-lebron.html.

FINLEY, BILL. "The LeBron James Show Is Coming to the End of Act I." *The New York Times*, 27 Mar. 2003, www.nytimes.com/2003/03/27/sports/pro -basketball-the-lebron-james-show-is-coming-to-the-end-of-act-i.html.

HOFFMAN, BENJAMIN. "LeBron James and Stephen Curry Unite Against White House Visits." *The New York Times*, 5 June 2018, www.nytimes .com/2018/06/05/sports/lebron-james-stephen-curry-trump.html.

HOFFMAN, BENJAMIN. "LeBron James Celebrates 30,000th Point and Then He Scores It." *The New York Times*, 23 Jan. 2018, https://www.nytimes .com/2018/01/23/sports/lebron-james-30000-points.html.

ITZKOFF, DAVE. "LeBron James and His Alter Egos Star in an Internet Animated Series." *The New York Times*, 17 Jan. 2011, www.nytimes.com /2011/01/18/arts/television/18lebron.html.

JENKINS, LEE. "Two Rookie Sensations Don't Make All-Star Cut." *The New York Times*, 4 Feb. 2004, www.nytimes.com/2004/02/04/sports/pro -basketball-two-rookie-sensations-don-t-make-all-star-cut.html.

LEITCH, WILL. "LeBron James and the Superstar Fallacy." *The New York Times*, 19 May 2018, www.nytimes.com/2018/05/19/opinion/lebron-james -nba-finals.html.

LEWIS, FRANK W. "A Statement Hits Home as Cleveland Stews." *The New York Times*, 9 July 2010, www.nytimes.com/2010/07/10/sports/basketball /10cavaliers.html.

LILLY, BRANDON. "It's Decisions, Decisions for LeBron James." *The New York Times*, 12 July 2002, www.nytimes.com/2002/07/12/sports/basketball -it-s-decisions-decisions-for-lebron-james.html.

LITSKY, FRANK. "LeBron James's S.U.V. Prompts an Investigation." *The New York Times*, 14 Jan. 2003, https://www.nytimes.com/2003/01/14/sports /basketball-lebron-james-s-suv-prompts-an-investigation.html.

MCGRATH, CHARLES. "N.B.A. Star, Now Memoirist, on Hometown Court." *The New York Times*, 4 Sept. 2009, www.nytimes.com/2009/09/05 /books/05lebron.html.

NOBLES, CHARLIE. "James Era Begins Before 15,123." *The New York Times*, 9 July 2003, www.nytimes.com/2003/07/09/sports/pro-basketball-james -era-begins-before-15123.html.

POWELL, MICHAEL. "Donald Trump and the Black Athlete." *The New York Times*, 5 Aug. 2018, www.nytimes.com/2018/08/05/sports/trump-lebron -james.html.

POWELL, MICHAEL. "LeBron James Delivered. Now Does He Exit?" *The*

New York Times, 7 June 2018, www.nytimes.com/2018/06/07/sports
/lebron-james-cleveland.html.

RHODEN, WILLIAM C. "Burden Unites the Cleveland Stars Jim Brown and
LeBron James." *The New York Times*, 9 June 2015, www.nytimes.com
/2015/06/10/sports/basketball/burden-unites-the-cleveland-stars
-jim-brown-and-lebron-james.html.

RHODEN, WILLIAM C. "Cleveland's Venom Validates James's Exit." *The New
York Times*, 9 July 2010, www.nytimes.com/2010/07/10/sports/basketball
/10rhoden.html.

RHODEN, WILLIAM C. "In Going Home, James May Be Ending an Exile From
Himself." *The New York Times*, 12 July 2014, www.nytimes.com/2014/07/13
/sports/basketball/in-going-home-lebron-james-may-be-ending-an-exile
-from-himself-.html.

RHODEN, WILLIAM C. "Young Guns Try Something New: Benchwarming."
The New York Times, 25 Aug. 2004, www.nytimes.com/2004/08/25/sports
/summer-2004-games-basketball-men-s-quarterfinals-young-guns-try
-something-new.html.

ROBBINS, LIZ. "James Is Earning His Wings." *The New York Times*, 21 Nov.
2004, www.nytimes.com/2004/11/21/sports/basketball/james-is-earning
-his-wings.html.

ROBERTS, SELENA. "LeBron Carnival Makes Its Debut." *The New York Times*,
30 Oct. 2003, www.nytimes.com/2003/10/30/sports/sports-of-the-times
-lebron-carnival-makes-its-debut.html.

STEIN, MARC. "LeBron James Returns to Cleveland, and Lakers Come Back
to Win." *The New York Times*, 21 Nov. 2018, www.nytimes.com/2018/11/21
/sports/lebron-james-lakers-cleveland-cavaliers.html.

STEIN, MARC. "LeBron James to the Lakers: There's Much to Unpack Here."
The New York Times, 2 July 2018, www.nytimes.com/2018/07/02/sports
/lebron-lakers.html.

STEIN, MARC. "The N.B.A. Has the Hottest Stove. LeBron James Is the Flame."
The New York Times, 30 June 2018, www.nytimes.com/2018/06/30/sports
/nba-free-agency-lebron-james.html.

STEIN, MARC, AND SCOTT CACCIOLA. "LeBron James Joining Lakers on 4-Year
$154 Million Deal." *The New York Times*, 1 July 2018, www.nytimes.com
/2018/07/01/sports/lebron-james-lakers.html.

STREETER, KURT. "LeBron James Puts on a Lakers Uniform, and a Stoic

Mask." *The New York Times*, 24 Sept. 2018, www.nytimes.com/2018/09/24
/sports/basketball/lebron-james-lakers.html.

TRACY, MARC. "The Arc of the LeBron James Story Reaches Its Climax."
The New York Times, 21 June 2016, www.nytimes.com/2016/06/22/sports
/basketball/lebron-james-nba-title-cleveland.html.

VORKUNOV, MIKE. "LeBron James Fires Back at Phil Jackson for 'Posse'
Comment." *The New York Times*, 15 Nov. 2016, www.nytimes.com/2016/11
/16/sports/basketball/lebron-james-phil-jackson-posse-comment.html.

WISE, MIKE. "Hoops in Hollywood, for Young Dreamers." *The New York
Times*, 5 Jan. 2003, www.nytimes.com/2003/01/05/sports/on-basketball
-hoops-in-hollywood-for-young-dreamers.html.

Index

This book is current up until the time of printing. For the most up-to-date reporting, visit www.nytimes.com.